Railways in Cleveland

60p.

Other Dalesman books on transport:

GEORGE HUDSON OF YORK.
THE M6: from Forton to Penrith
MAIN LINE OVER SHAP
NAVIGABLE RIVERS OF YORKSHIRE
RAILWAYS IN THE NORTH
RAILWAYS IN THE PEAK DISTRICT
SETTLE–CARLISLE RAILWAY
TRACTION ENGINES IN THE NORTH
TRANSPORT IN YORKSHIRE
WHITBY–PICKERING RAILWAY
YORKSHIRE PORTS AND HARBOURS

Railways in Cleveland

by

K. Hoole

DALESMAN BOOKS
1971

DALESMAN PUBLISHING COMPANY LTD.,
CLAPHAM (via Lancaster). Yorkshire.
First Published 1971

ISBN: 0 85206 131 5

Printed and bound in Great Britain by
FRETWELL & BRIAN LTD.
Silsden, Nr. Keighley, Yorkshire.

Contents

The cover illustrations show:- Front: Diesel unit on 9.55a.m. Middlesbrough-Whitby off-loads hikers at Kildale on a summer Sunday, June 18th, 1966 (John Boyes). Back, upper: Class P locomotive No. 1822 on train of ironstone wagons near Great Ayton about 1910 (British Railways). Back, lower: Lewin-built locomotive and a group of ironstone miners at Great Ayton, about 1900 (photographer unknown).

The title page line drawing of a train on the Rosedale branch is by P. D. Stoddart. All uncredited photographs in the text are by the author.

Introduction

FOR many years the Cleveland area, in the north east corner of Yorkshire, played a very important part in the development of the iron and steel industry. This was brought about by the discovery of a plentiful supply of iron ore in the Cleveland hills, and also by the foresight of the directors of the Stockton & Darlington Railway and the Pease family, who decided to build a dock at Middlesbrough, further down river from the original terminus at Stockton Wharf. With iron ore on the doorstep and coal not very far away, the area became the centre of the iron making industry in north eastern England. Mines and ironworks thrived together but the import of superior foreign ores eventually displaced that produced by the Cleveland mines and, one after the other, they closed down until the last, at North Skelton, ceased operations in January 1964.

Iron ore was also supplied to ironworks built nearer the coal seams, such as those at Tudhoe, Tow Law, Consett and Ferryhill, although the latter works were actually supplied from mines in Rosedale, on the extreme edge of the Cleveland field and some fifteen miles away to the south from the centre of the ironstone mining industry at Guisborough.

It required a fascinating railway to reach Rosedale, without which the ore would never have got to Ferryhill, and it seems unlikely that the line would have been built if it wasn't for the fact that two of the partners in the Ferryhill Ironworks were high officials of the North Eastern Railway. To reach the crest of the Cleveland hills the railway required a massive rope-worked incline, and because of its exposed and remote position the Rosedale branch has long fascinated the railway enthusiast. But, for the same reasons, it was an extremely difficult line to reach as the nearest passenger station was at Battersby, more than 2½ miles from the foot of the incline, while at the other end of the line the terminus at West Rosedale was seven miles from Sinnington station on the N.E.R. Pickering to Gilling branch. Consequently it was not until the motor car age that the Rosedale branch was really accessible —and by then it was in its decline, or had actually closed and been dismantled.

However, one enthusiast who did visit the line as early as 1903 was the late J. Hayes of Gateshead, who managed to obtain photographs of the line at work, with the former Stockton & Darlington Class 1001 0-6-0 engines at the head of the trains. Twenty-five years later another photographer, strangely enough also called Hayes, photographed trains on the line, and also the equipment installed to work and load the calcined ore from the gigantic heaps which had accumulated near the kilns. Fortunately the negatives of the latter collection are still in existence. Photographs were also taken pre-1914 by J. W. Brotton when he was the Weigh Office Clerk at Incline Foot: he later retired as stationmaster at Pinchinthorpe.

Articles and notes on the Rosedale branch have appeared in the *Railway Observer,* the *Railway Magazine,* and other periodicals, and the *Scarborough Archaeological Society* has published a duplicated booklet on the line. These, together with the Leeman and other papers at the British Transport Historical Records Office at York, have been studied in producing the following account of the line, which contains details previously unpublished. Because of the great interest in the railway it has been covered in some detail.

For details of other railways in Cleveland I am indebted to the extensive collection of records kept by the North Eastern Railway and its successors, now in the custody of the British Transport Historical Records Office at York, where Mr. W. J. MacDonald has afforded every assistance, and also to my co-explorer T. E. Rounthwaite. His articles in the *Railway Observer* on the railways of Cleveland have, I know, interested many people and set them off tramping the hills of Cleveland to explore some of the long-closed mines and branches.

Much of the early railway development in Cleveland was due to the Stockton & Darlington Railway as the power behind the Middlesbrough & Guisborough Railway, and a competitor was the short-lived Cleveland Railway. The North Eastern Railway at first only had the Rosedale branch, but by successively taking over the North Yorkshire & Cleveland Railway, the Stockton & Darlington Railway, and the Cleveland Railway, between 1858 and 1865, it acquired the whole of the railway system in Cleveland.

Since then the ironstone mining industry has flourished and died, although Teesside is still an important centre for iron and steel. In the last fifty years the area has been further

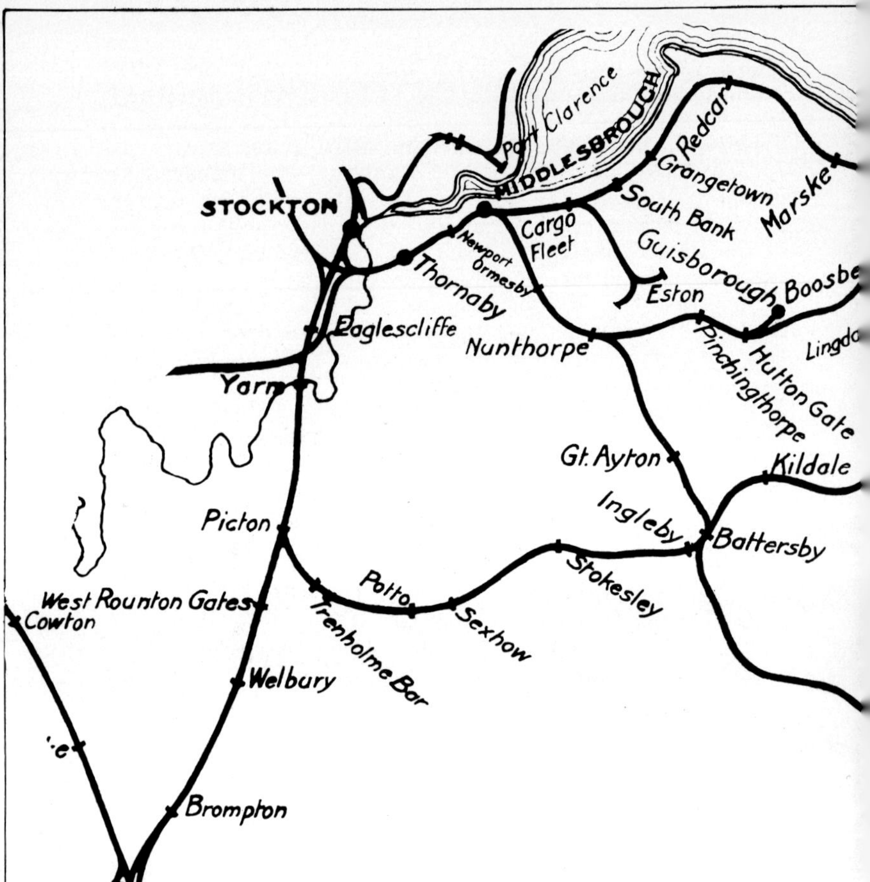

Railways in Cleveland:

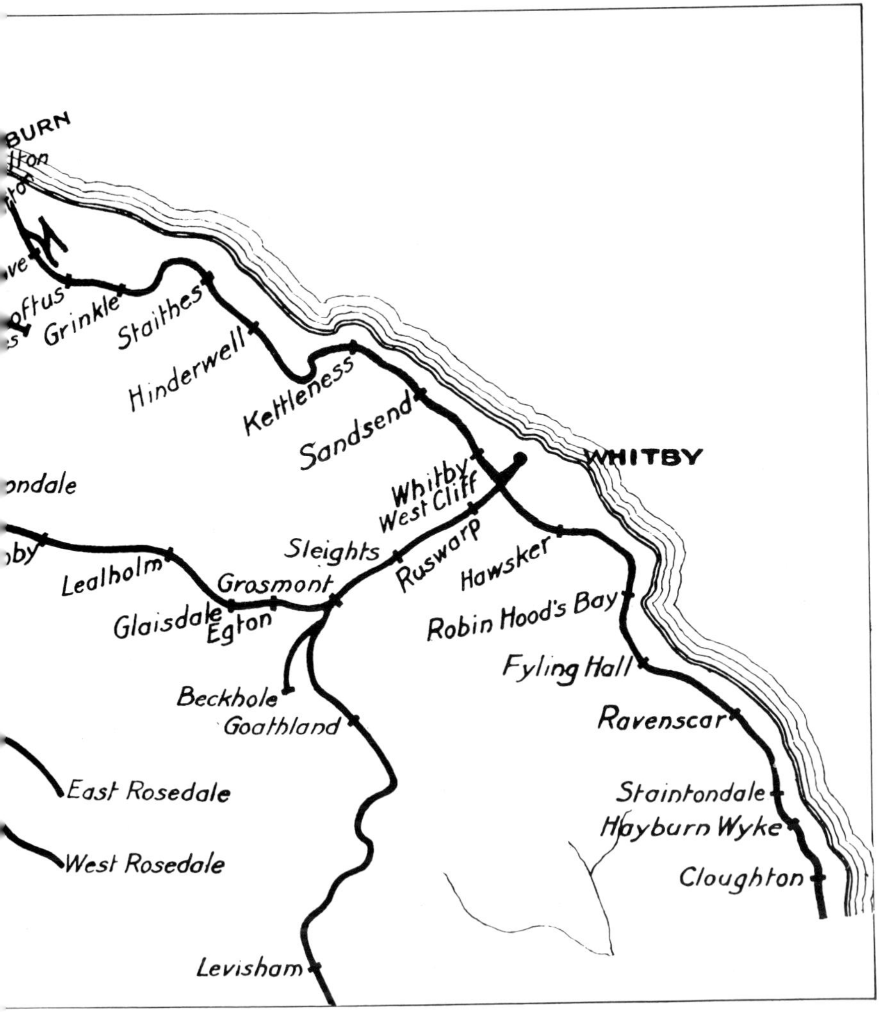

Scale about 5 miles to an inch

industrialised by the I.C.I. complex of chemical plants on both sides of the river Tees. Fortunately for the historian, other industries have not generally spread over the sites of the various mines, and much is still to be seen of this once thriving industry. However, a good map is necessary, preferably an old one, when exploring the mines and their railways and this can make an interesting and educational pastime, particularly if the weather is fine and you are able to enjoy the Cleveland countryside at its best.

Class P locomotive No. 1860 at Blowith Crossing (R. Hayes).

1: Rosedale

IN 1873, just less than a century ago, the mines at Rosedale turned out 560,668 tons of ironstone, or 1,500 tons *per day!* This was the peak year for Rosedale ironstone and at six shillings per ton the output for 1873 was valued at £168,200. However, with the failure of the Rosedale & Ferryhill Iron Company Ltd. in 1879 the mines were closed, and although they did reopen the output never again reached the massive figures for 1873. In fact by 1879 the price of ironstone was falling rapidly and in 1880 and 1881 it was only three shillings a ton, or half of what it had been less than a decade earlier.

The first signs of large scale mining in Rosedale were in 1856, when George Leeman, Alexander Clunes Sheriff and Isaac Hartas formed the Rosedale Mining Company and took the lease of some land at Rosedale Abbey owned by Thomas Garbutt. George Leeman was the deputy chairman of the North Eastern Railway (and later chairman), Member of Parliament for York, and one time chief enemy of George Hudson. A. C. Sheriff was the goods manager of the York & North Midland Railway, and he became passenger manager of the NER on its formation in 1854: he later became Member of Parliament for Worcester and a director of several railway companies, including the Metropolitan and the Metropolitan District. Mr. Sheriff resigned from the NER on 11 July 1856.

In 1856, 1857 and 1858 ironstone was mined and samples were sent to various ironworks for trial purposes: these included works at Leeds and Masborough, and the firms of Gilkes Wilson & Co., South Durham Co., and Consett Iron Co.; the latter received 7,073 tons and paid £3,713 11s. 0d. for it. The ore proved to be of excellent quality and in 1859 a sixty year lease was taken on a further 8,000 acres from Henry Brewster Darley, who received a royalty of sixpence per ton. At this time there was no railway nearer than Pickering, ten miles away, and until 1861 all the ironstone had to be carted by road to Pickering and it then had to travel by rail by a roundabout route via Malton, Gilling and Pilmoor to reach the blast furnaces at Middlesbrough and in County Durham.

Once the Rosedale Mining Co. had established that there was workable ore, and that it was of suitable quality, the company approached the NER about providing railway access. The North Eastern deputed Professor Phillips and Nicholas Wood to make an extensive survey, referring more particularly to the extent of the ironstone: borings were to be undertaken by the Mining Co. Professor Phillips and Nicholas Wood commenced their survey in July 1857 and they must have taken their task very seriously and thoroughly as their report was not submitted to the NER Board until October 1858. Unfortunately a copy of this report has not been located but an earlier reference was made to seams "upwards of thirty feet thick." On 15 October 1858 the NER Board of Directors approved the construction of the Rosedale branch, with the instruction that the line should be staked out. The estimated cost was £50,000 and at the same time it was decided to apply for powers to purchase the Rosedale branch of the North Yorkshire & Cleveland Railway.

Ironstone mining in Cleveland was already spreading southwards and on 6 April 1858 a private narrow gauge railway owned by the Ingleby Ironstone & Freestone Mining Co. was opened from Burton Head to join the North Yorkshire & Cleveland line near Ingleby. At this time the NY&C was extending steadily eastwards from Picton Junction on the Northallerton-Stockton line of the former Leeds Northern Railway: Picton to Stokesley was opened for traffic on 3 March 1857, but east of Stokesley the opening to Ingleby on 1 February 1858, and on to Kildale on 6 April 1858 was for mineral traffic only. Passenger traffic east of Stokesley did not commence until the line reached Castleton in April 1861.

The NY&C was built under three Acts of Parliament; the first, which received the Royal Assent on 10 July 1854, authorised the line from Picton to Grosmont. The second (Royal Assent 2 July 1855) authorised the branch from Ingleby Junction (Battersby) to Nunthorpe Junction on the Middlesbrough & Guisborough Railway, and a branch from Potto to Whorlton to serve ironstone mines. The third Act (Royal Assent 23 July 1858) granted powers to purchase the Ingleby Private Branch Railway and to extend the railway to Three Hoes (Three Howes) at Rosedale West: it also authorised the NER to take over the NY&C which it did from 1 January 1859. For some reason the powers to build the Rosedale branch were not transferred under this Act, but were treated

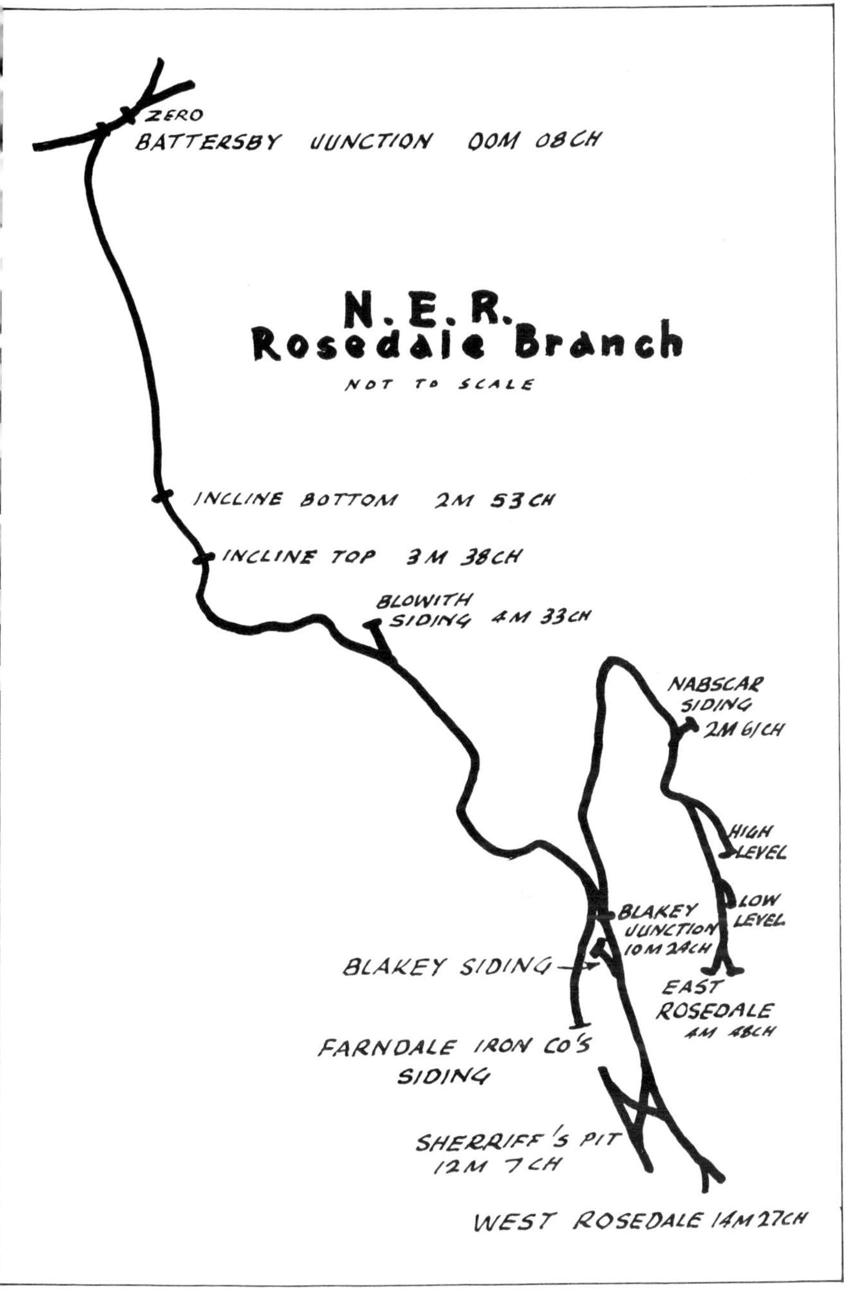

N.E.R.
Rosedale Branch
NOT TO SCALE
ZERO
BATTERSBY JUNCTION 00M 08CH
INCLINE BOTTOM 2M 53CH
INCLINE TOP 3M 38CH
BLOWITH SIDING 4M 33CH
NABSCAR SIDING 2M 61CH
HIGH LEVEL
LOW LEVEL
BLAKEY JUNCTION 10M 24CH
BLAKEY SIDING
EAST ROSEDALE 4M 48CH
FARNDALE IRON CO'S SIDING
SHERRIFF'S PIT 12M 7CH
WEST ROSEDALE 14M 27CH

separately in an Act of 8 August 1859, vesting the Rosedale branch in the NER.

The NER had worked the NY&C from the outset through its takeover of the Leeds Northern. The West Hartlepool Harbour & Railway Co. also had a stake in the NY&C and was behind the Cleveland Railway from the Tees, southwards to Guisborough and Skinningrove, which actually received an Act for the construction of the Guisborough-Skinningrove section on the same day as the third NY&C Act, namely 23 July 1858. No doubt because of their common interest in the NY&C, the NY&C Act of 23 July 1858 contained a clause covering the working of NER ironstone traffic to Ferryhill via the West Hartlepool line, presumably over their former Clarence Railway route through Sedgefield. However, by the time the Rosedale branch was opened in 1861, the NER were not prepared to take advantage of the above clause. On 5 April 1861, Edward Fletcher, the NER locomotive superintendent, reported that he had reached agreement with William Bouch of the Stockton & Darlington Railway for the latter company's engines to work the traffic between Rosedale and Ferryhill, presumably via Allen's Curve at Eaglescliffe and the Ironstone Curve in the north-east angle of the Stockton & Darlington crossing at Darlington. For locomotive power the NER agreed to pay to the S&D ¼d per train mile.

It is obvious that this activity centred on getting a route from Rosedale to Ferryhill and no doubt the various negotiations were helped along by George Leeman, both in his capacity as deputy chairman of the North Eastern and a partner in the Rosedale Mining Co. Incidentally, the latter company became a limited liability company on 18 June 1864 under the new title of The Rosedale & Ferryhill Iron Co. Ltd. and erected large ironworks at Ferryhill, but failed in January 1879, bringing to an end their Rosedale activities and temporary closure of the mines.

On 29 July 1859 the NER Board instructed Mr. Harrison, the engineer, to have plans and specifications of the Rosedale branch completed by 1 September and to advertise for tenders for the construction of the branch, the tenders to be returned by 9-0 a.m. on 23 September. Obviously time was short but a number of tenders were received by the due date and that of P. Stuart was accepted at £19,734 0s. 8d. subject to satisfactory references. Mr. Harrison later reported that as far as he could ascertain Mr. Stuart was a suitable contractor but on 20 January 1860 he reported to the Board that Stuart was unable to fulfil the contract and it had been awarded to (and accepted by) Mr. R. Cail at £24,500.

The task was finished in March 1861, involving the conversion of the Ingleby Mining Company's line to standard gauge, the construction of the notable Ingleby Incline, and the laying of track across 10½ miles of wild, bleak moorland. The work could have been completed earlier if only the weather had been better but the unfavourable conditions, together with some landslips, delayed work and the contractor was put to extra expense for which he had not allowed. Consequently on 4 October 1861 Mr. Cail approached the NER with the request that he be paid an extra £4,000. Mr. Harrison was called upon to prepare a report on the matter and in the following month Mr. Cail was granted an additional payment of £2,000.

Part of the line ran over the land of Lord de L'Isle and on 15 December 1860 the NER agreed to pay his Lordship a royalty based on traffic passing over the line, the maximum payment being £530 a year and the minimum £330 a year. In the meantime authority had been given for the building of 300 new eight ton iron hopper-shaped wagons for working the ironstone traffic on the Rosedale branch. These were necessary because it was planned to calcine the ore at Rosedale and when loaded it would still be hot. By heating the ore in the kilns the moisture content was expelled and thus the mineral was lightened in weight, reducing the wayleaves payable. These wagons became Dgm.S1 in the NER Wagon Diagram Book.

On 13 April 1860 a shed for three engines, and a small fitting shop, were authorised to be erected at Rosedale West at an estimated cost of £500. It was stipulated that a tender for the building should be obtained from the contractor for the line, Mr. Cail, and on 11 May 1860 his tender for £760 was accepted. No doubt the shed was completed in time for the opening of the line on 27 March 1861, but in the following year Mr. Fletcher was applying for permission to enlarge the shed. On 26 September 1862 plans for the extension were submitted, together with plans for a 'blacksmith's shop and these were approved. A couple of weeks later a tender of £330 15s. 0d. was accepted, but by the end of March 1863 the job had not been completed as the contractor had gone bankrupt and the next lowest tender of £334 was accepted. However, the extensions were completed by the end of the year and actually cost £18 10s. 3d. less than authorised. The shed was a two-road stone built structure, which officially closed on 24 January 1929, when the last two engines were transferred away.

West Rosedale. This page, top: The kilns, August 9th, 1966. This page, bottom: Looking down the course of the incline to the original mines, March 29th, 1959. Opposite: General view about 1911 with engine shed on left, two snowploughs in centre and N.E.R. cottages on right. (R. Hayes).

The building remained empty until the 1930s but it was then demolished and the stones utilised to build the village hall at Hutton-le-Hole, some three miles away.

While the Rosedale branch was under construction the contractor was short of men for working in this exposed area and to speed the work the NER agreed to affix posters to their wagons. These read:- "WANTED: a number of GOOD MASONS, Quarrymen and Navvies. Wages: Masons 5s. 0d. to 6s. 0d; Quarrymen 4s. 6d. to 5s. 6d.; Navvies 3s. 4d. to 4s. 9d. Apply Foreman on Works, Rosedale." One of these notices was affixed to a wagon by the porter at Pensher (later Penshaw) and this wagon found its way into a nearby quarry owned by the Londonderry family, where the men were on strike for shorter hours. This led to a letter of protest from the Londonderry offices at Seaham Harbour to the Secretary of the NER, protesting about the 'poaching' of their men.

On June 24th 1864 the NER Board was informed that the Rosedale Mining Co. (which had actually become the Rosedale & Ferryhill Iron Co. Ltd. eight days earlier) was to open workings at East Rosedale and that rail connection was desired with the West Rosedale line. It was immediately agreed that the Mining Co. should make the line (to Mr. Harrison's satisfaction) and that the NER should take it over at cost. On 28 October Mr. Harrison was instructed to prepare plans for the line and it was opened on 18 August 1865. In the meantime the NER had obtained an Act to build the line which cost the company £7,562 2s 11d, and George Leeman was paid £7,500 'on account'. An Ordnance Survey map in the York collection of the BRB Historical Records Office has the Rosedale branches inked in and shows a curve between the East Rosedale branch and the Blakey Junction to Incline Top line but this was not built.

Production from the East and West mines totalled some 250,000 tons in 1865, and with the completion of the link between Castleton and Grosmont, the North Yorkshire & Cleveland Branch warranted a new and fuller table in the Working Timetable for October 1865, with the heading changed to Stockton and Whitby. This table included for the first time the Rosedale ironstone trains, whereas previously only those from Potto (off the Whorlton and Swainby branch) had been shown. The Rosedale service was:—

	* a.m.	a.m.	a.m.	p.m.
Darlington	—	6–0	8–0	1–0
Stockton	6–0	—	—	—
Picton Junction	6–35	7–0	8–55	1–45
Ingleby	7–15	7–40	9–40	2–25

	a.m.	a.m.	p.m.	* p.m.
Ingleby	10–15	11–41	4–35	4–50
Picton Junction	11–10	12–35	5–25	5–35
Stockton	—	—	—	6–10
Darlington	—	—	—	—

* = Engine employed during the day working ironstone on the Ingleby Branch.

The timings at Ferryhill cannot be ascertained with certainty but at least three of the four trains were worked via Darlington, and probably the fourth also ran that way after staging at Stockton overnight.

The North Eastern absorbed the West Hartlepool Harbour & Railway under an Act of 5 July 1865 and the WTT for November 1865 shows all the Rosedale ironstone trains travelling via Stockton and Sedgefield, as intended originally under the clause in the 1858 Act. Times became:—

		*			
	a.m.	a.m.	a.m.	a.m.	p.m.
Ferryhill	—	—	8–0	11–0	3–30
Stockton	5–0	6–0	9–45	12–45	4–45
Picton Junction	5–25	6–35	10–15	1–0	—
Ingleby	6–15	7–15	11–00	1–45	—

					*
	a.m.	a.m.	a.m.	p.m.	p.m.
Ingleby	—	6–45	11–45	2–45	4–50
Picton Junction	—	7–30	12–25	3–40	5–35
Stockton	5–20	8–0	1–10	4–15	6–0
Ferryhill	7–0	10–0	2–45	—	—

* = Engine to work on Ingleby Branch.

It seems probable that the 5–0 a.m. from Stockton, the 6–45 a.m. from Ingleby, the 11–0 a.m. from Ferryhill and the 2–45 from Ingleby was one turn, worked by a single set of men, and the 5–20 a.m. from Stockton, the 8–0 a.m. from Ferryhill, the 11–45 a.m. from Ingleby, and the 3–30 p.m. from Ferryhill was another similar turn. The 6–0 a.m. from Stockton and the 4–50 p.m. from Ingleby is specifically quoted as one turn, and all three gave the men a day of well over twelve hours when the preparing and stabling times are taken into account. It was these long hours which led to the enginemen's strike of 1867, when they were fighting for a ten hour day on running engines and a twelve hour day on shunting and piloting engines.

In 1873, the peak year for Rosedale traffic, the service was:—

		*						
	a.m	a.m.	a.m.	a.m.	a.m.	p.m.	p.m.	p.m.
Ferryhill	—	—	—	7–40	10–10	12–10	3–20	4–15
Stockton	4–50	5–10	6–45	9–45	12–25	2–0	4–45	5–25
Ingleby	6–0	6–20	8–0	11–0	1–40	3–10	—	—

	a.m.	a.m.	a.m.	a.m.	p.m.	p.m.	p.m.
Ingleby	—	—	8–30	11–40	12–40	2–20	3–40
Stockton	4–35	5–20	9–50	1–5	1–55	3–25	4–50
Ferryhill	6–0	6–40	11–10	2–20	3–15	+	+

* = Shunt and work Ingleby branch and return with load when work is finished.

+ = To work through to Ferryhill if required.

Although the loads were smaller and the gradients not so severe, the service is reminiscent of that provided years later to get the same product—ironstone—from Tyne Dock to Consett using 9F 2–10–0s!

After the failure of the Rosedale & Ferryhill Iron Co. Ltd. the mines at Rosedale and the ironworks at Ferryhill were both taken over by the Carlton Iron Co. Thus it seems probable that when they relit the furnaces the ironstone would resume its original route via Picton and, in fact, it has not been possible to trace the ironstone travelling to Middlesbrough by the Great Ayton route at any period. However, it does seem likely that the ore first obtained at Ingleby by the Ingleby Mining Co. was intended for the blast furnaces on the south side of the river Tees, for their line made for the NY&C just short of the spot where the proposed branch to join the Middlesbrough & Guisborough Railway was to diverge. The despatch of the Rosedale ore to Ferryhill, which could be sent via Picton, rendered this line unnecessary and it was not built immediately. As the NER were showing no signs of building the line, the Stockton & Darlington Railway (which had taken over the Middlesbrough & Guisborough Railway in 1858) wanted to construct it and the matter was referred to arbitration. Thus it was decided that the NER should make the line, but it was not opened until 1 June 1864 (for mineral traffic) and 1 April 1868 (for passenger traffic). The curve at the south end for traffic from the Grosmont direction to the Great Ayton direction was not built, and neither was the curve at the north end, from the Guisborough direction to the Great Ayton direction.

The engines in use at Rosedale shed in the early days were short-wheelbase ("long-boilered") 0–6–0s, which were later known as Class 93 on the NER. Nos. 422 and 423, both built by Robert Stephenson & Co. in 1860, were there in 1867 and they were followed by Nos. 564, 571 and 580 of the same class but built by Hawthorn & Co. in 1866. Once an engine went to Rosedale it was usual for it to stay there for some years, due to the trouble involved in getting locomotives up and down the incline. Consequently, considering its size, large repairs had to be done at Rosedale shed, and to save an engine going to the works for wheel turning Mr. Fletcher was authorised to purchase a spare set of locomotive wheels from Stephenson & Co. in 1861 at a cost of £342, presumably for Nos. 422 and 423.

The next class of engine known to have worked at Rosedale was the famous long-boilered 0–6–0 of Stockton & Darlington origin, designed by William Bouch. One of this class is preserved in the Railway Museum at York. Engines known to have been at Rosedale at one time or another were Nos. 1108, 1126, 1128, 1129, 1192, 1193, 1195, 1255, 1282 and 1286. The three 12xx engines were the last of the class at Rosedale and they disappeared from the scene in 1919. Another engine at this remote shed was class 1196 0–6–0 1756, originally built in 1866 as a 0–6–0ST for working the Skinningrove zig-zag but later rebuilt as a 0–6–0 tender engine; this engine was withdrawn from Rosedale on 27 August 1908.

From 1915 to 1919 McDonnell 0–6–0 1489 was at Rosedale shed. Although Darlington Works' records listed a drawing for a weather-board or cab on the tender of this engine there is no proof that it was ever fitted, although it was the practice to fit tender cabs on the Rosedale engines. Photographs exist of the Stockton & Darlington engines, and the later Class P 0–6–0, all fitted. The three Class P 0–6–0s, 1860, 1893 and 1950, went to Rosedale in 1919 and 1920, and 1950 was the first to leave when it was transferred to Saltburn on 22 August 1927. The other two stayed on after the line closed to help with the dismantling and although both were transferred to Saltburn on 24 January 1929 when Rosedale shed officially closed, 1893 remained until the demolition was completed in June 1929. It is possible that 1893 was brought down the incline earlier but had to be returned as the 0–4–0 ST provided by the demolition contractors was unsuitable for the work. Mr. W. Huby, who was stationmaster and goods agent at Battersby at the time, recalls that a crew provided by the contractor were passed to drive 1893 on its demolition duties. These three engines were eventually withdrawn as follows:—

1860 from York in November 1951 as 5619.
1893 from Middlesbrough in October 1938.
1950 withdrawn in April 1939 but re-instated and finally withdrawn from Tyne Dock in October 1945.

Normally when an engine had to be lowered down the incline, it had the centre pair of coupled wheels removed at Rosedale shed and was worked to the Incline Top. It was then lowered down, on only four wheels. This was done for two reasons; firstly so that the crank axle did not foul the rope sheaves, and secondly because of the change of gradient at the top of the incline. Going over the top, a six-wheeled engine would have the leading wheels in mid-air when the centre and rear pair of wheels were still on the level, and then as it moved forward and overbalanced the leading and centre pairs of wheels would have been on the incline rails and the rear pair up in the air, until the engine ran forward far enough to get all its wheels on the incline. At the foot of the incline the change of gradient would have left the engine standing on the leading and rear pairs of wheels, with the centre wheels up in the air. Consequently, when 0–6–0 1893 had worked all the lifted track to Incline Top it had to be jacked up and packed so that the crank axle and centre pair of wheels could be removed before it could be safely lowered down. At the shed sheer legs had been provided for such an operation.

The incline itself was 1,430 yds. long and the wire rope used for haulage was one inch diameter and 1,650 yds. long. By Act of Parliament the NER was allowed to charge double rate on goods passing up and down the incline; thus the rate for 1 mile 50 chains was charged instead of the actual 65 chains. The gradient on the incline was 1 in 11 at the bottom, then 1 in 8, 1 in 6, and finally 1 in 5 approaching the summit. As usual with self-acting inclines there was a single track at the foot of the incline, 542 yds. long; two separate tracks at the meetings or passing place, 160 yds.; and three rails on the top section, 638 yds. long. On the three-rail section the centre rail was common to the alternately descending and ascending wagons. At the very top of the incline the three rails branched into three tracks, the centre one continued on a steady gradient and passed under the drums in the drumhouse. This was for the descending wagons. The two tracks on either side went over an artificial summit built up of stones, so that once they were over the crest the wagons ran down the slope to safety instead of being liable to run back down the incline. The arangement of tracks at the summit was known as the "kip." Care had to be exercised when the wagons were running along this short stretch at the top and they had to be brought to a stand by putting sprags in the wheels. If allowed to go too far the leading wagon could be hoisted into the air as the rope rose to pass on to the drum.

The ascending wagons were also protected by a safety device which consisted of a short length of rail in the centre of the track, pivoted just off centre so that its upper end was depressed by the axles of the wagons. After each axle passed over, the rail end lifted again so that it could provide an obstruction to any wagon tending to run back down the incline if, for instance, the brakesman brought the wagons to a stand before the ascending set had all passed safely on to the kip. A similar arrangement was usually provided for descending wagons, but in this case it was manually operated so that it could be depressed when the descending wagons were ready to start their downward run.

In spite of these precautions, wagons did occasionally get

Ingleby Incline. Top: Drum house at summit, showing metal bodied hopper wagons for carrying "roasted" ore while still hot (R. Hayes).
Bottom: View down incline, August 20th, 1957.

away out of control, either by a mistake on the part of the staff, or because of the breakage of the rope or a wagon coupling. Trap points leading to runaway sidings were provided on each side immediately below the point where the three tracks went into three rails, and at the bottom of the double track section, just before the two tracks went into one. A man was stationed at the lower points when the incline was running, but the top points were operated by one of the men handling the wagons at the top of the incline. However, wagons did occasionally get amain and there is a photograph in existence of the wreckage caused by some wagons which ran away and crashed into others standing in the sidings at the foot of

OUTPUT OF IRONSTONE AT ROSEDALE 1861-1881

Year	West Mines Tons	East Mines Tons	Total Tons	Remarks
1861	79,786	—	79,786	Roasted 27,686 tons Unroasted 52,100 tons Total value £11,967 18s.
1862	219,123	—	219,123	Value £32,768 0s. 0d.
1863	224,889	—	224,889	
1864	297,579	—	297,579	Value £66,950 0s. 0d.
1865	250,000	—	250,000	Estimated value £62,510 0s. 0d.
1866	61,643	168,739	230,382	Total value £93,490 0s 0d.
1867	??	??	178,227	
1868	??	??	210,082	
1869	??	??	269,595	
1870	??	??	317,060	
1871	??	??	314,394	
1872	??	??	450,350	
1873	??	??	560,668	Value £168,200 0s. 0d.
1874	??	??	473,140	Value £141,942 0s. 0d.
1875	79,306	292,326	371,632	
1876	103,722	266,422	383,827	Includes 13,683 tons from Sherriff's Pit
1877	85,685	258,801	344,486	
1878	55,245	178,905	234,150	
1879	6,874	18,718	25,592	Mines closed from March
1880	—	—	—	
1881	—	—	6,079	Sherriff's Pit reopened

the incline. Needless to say the result was a pile of splintered wood and miscellaneous metal fittings.

Because of the position of the drumhouse, wagons going down the incline were restricted to a height of 9ft 6 in above rail level: thus only open wagons were to be found on the top section of the branch. Special arrangements had to be made to lower the engines, brakevans and snowploughs and they had to depart from one of the ascending kips. Trolley wagons and six-wheel wagons could not be worked on the incline and another restriction covered the height from rail to the underside of loads, which had to be not less than fourteen inches.

In the drumhouse the two drums were mounted side by side on a common shaft: on one drum the rope ran on to the top of the drum and on the other on to the bottom, so that as they revolved one drum was winding in the rope as the other was paying it out. The drums were controlled by a brakesman stationed in a building at the crest of the incline: a treadle was fixed on the three-rail section so that the ascending wagons operated a bell and in darkness or fog indicated their whereabouts to the brakesman. On 4 June 1869, Mr. Fletcher reported that the drumhouse had been destroyed by fire and that traffic up and down the incline had been suspended: this may have been due to the overheating of the brake bands. However, it was suggested that in future two drumhouses should be provided to provide against such a thing happening again and two additional drums were authorised, but these appear to have been erected in the one drumhouse, behind the working pair of drums.

* * * *

The first mines were established near Hollins Farm, south of the village of Rosedale Abbey, and the stone had to be hauled up to the NER terminus at West Rosedale by a winding engine. Presumably this was owned by the Rosedale Mining Co., although the appointment of a NER stationary engine fireman in 1883 at the age of fifteen poses a mystery. The Mining Company's narrow gauge line passed under the Rosedale Bank road and the bridge is still there, now filled in. The winding engine chimney, which has been allowed to remain, has been a landmark for more than a century. At the foot of the chimney the bed of the winding engine can be discerned and looking down the bank the course of the line can easily be seen as it winds down the side of the valley. Below the winding engine are the remains of the bank of kilns used to calcine the ore by heating it. This process expelled the water content of the ore, reducing the royalty payable on the ore sent to Ferryhill but leaving behind a quantity of unwanted dust, which was simply tipped into the valley out of the way. However, just before the line closed a use was found for this dust, which was rich in iron oxide, and it was reclaimed and sent to Teesside. This will be dealt with later.

In the first full year of operation the West mines produced 219,123 tons of ironstone worth £32,768 and in 1864 achieved a record output of 297,580 tons worth £66,950. However, only two years later the output was down to 61,643 tons (£18,490) but it picked up again in 1873/4, only to fall gradually from that date. These mines closed in 1879 with the failure of the Rosedale & Ferryhill Iron Co. Ltd. but reopened again, only to close for good in 1885.

The NER two-road engine shed was a few hundred yards north of the winding engine and the brick floor and filled-in inspection pits can still be found. The sheer legs for lifting the locomotives were outside the shed at the south end, and the coaling stage and crane were outside at the north end. Two miles north was Sherriff's Pit, named after one of the partners in the Mining Company, and this appears to have opened in 1876. In this case a vertical shaft was sunk 270 ft whereas at all the other sites the ironstone was obtained by drifts going into the hillside. However, at Sherriff's Pit there was also a drift going in from the hillside to the foot of the shaft, a distance of some 500 yds. The output in the first (incomplete) year was only 13,683 tons, whereas as in the full year the East and West mines produced 370,144 tons. There were no kilns at Sherriff's Pit and the ore was loaded direct into NER wagons. The mine closed in 1911 and a number of ruined buildings remain around the top of the shaft which still pierces the moor, protected by a fence to stop the moorland sheep and careless humans from falling down.

Over at the East mines some signs of the drift entrances, now blocked up, can still be located among the extensive remains of the workings. The ore was originally calcined at a bank of sixteen kilns a few hundred yards north of the East Rosedale terminus, but later three large kilns were erected about half a mile further north. In their first full year, 1866, the East mines produced 168,739 tons (worth £75,000) and the output gradually increased to a peak in 1873, when the East and West output reached 560,668 tons, with the output from the East mines double what it had been seven years previously.

After the failure of the Rosedale & Ferryhill Iron Co. Ltd. in 1879, the East mines were taken over by the Carlton Iron Co., together with Sherriff's Pit, and both continued in operation until 1911, when the Carlton Iron Co. closed down its operations in Rosedale. The East mines were taken over in 1912 by two partners, F. J. H. Lascelles (who had been manager of Sherriff's Pit under the Carlton Iron Co.) and J. Shepherd: on 1 February 1912 they signed an agreement with the NER, "To work with all convenience and speed the remaining ironstone in the East Rosedale mines, using their best ability to send down the Rosedale branch not less than 100,000 tons per year." The NER agreed to give six months' notice if they wished to close the line, but could close it at one month's notice if traffic fell below 6,000 tons per month.

At the same time the NER revised the amount of wayleave payable to Lord de L'Isle under the agreements of 1860 and 1865. Instead of the exisiting minimum payment of £330 a year and maximum of £530 a year, the new minimum was £314 for 100,000 tons or less, with payment at ½d per ton over this amount, to the same maximum of £530 per annum. The agreement between the NER and the Lascelles/Shepherd partnership was transferred to J. Shepherd and H. A. Pringle on 1 March 1919. Lascelles and Shepherd did reach their target in 1913 and 1914, and again in 1918, but in the 1920s output fell rapidly and it was down to only 9,233 tons in 1924: production ceased in the following year.

In 1917 a trial load of 154 tons of the calcine dust was despatched to see if a use could be found for it. It is not known where the dust went but presumably to one of the ironworks on Teesside. Although none went out in 1918 or 1919, it started to flow again in 1920 until in 1924 45,779 tons of dust were despatched. Altogether 231,504 tons of this by-product or waste travelled over the NER between 1920 and 1927. Over the years the dust had been tipped below the three sets of kilns and formed quite sizeable mounds. When it was found that the dust could be sold, tramways were laid from the dust heaps to hoppers mounted on gantries above the NER tracks. The dust was hauled up the tramway in tubs, tipped into the hoppers, and loaded into NER wagons standing in sidings provided for T. W. Ward Ltd. under an agreement dated 29 October 1919.

At the turn of the century the Carlton Iron Co. installed an electric generating plant at the East mines, supplied with steam generated by a boiler from the old winding engine at West Rosedale. The tubs were hauled out of the drifts by electric motors and electric lighting replaced the flickering candles and oil lamps, but this equipment was removed when the Carlton Iron Co. relinquished the mines in 1911.

A narrow gauge line ran beyond the NER terminus at East Rosedale to serve outcrop and quarry workings on the face of the escarpment. It passed under the main road (Knott Road) and continued to serve further workings in North Dale. The line was over a mile in length and most of the rock shelf on which it ran can still be located, although the tunnel under the road has disappeared. It is not clear when the line opened but two 3ft. 0in. gauge locomotives were purchased for the line in 1873: *Rosedale* was built by Manning , Wardle & Co., works number 475, and *Emily* by Black, Hawthorn & Co., works number 259. Both were 0-4-0ST with outside cylinders. They were both sold and left Rosedale when the Rosedale & Ferryhill Iron Co. Ltd. closed down in 1879. Near the course of the narrow gauge line the NER goods shed still stands, in quite good condition, but the stone coal cells are derelict: on the hillside just below the cells is the house formerly occupied by the NER goods agent, although for many years the coal passing through the cells was sold to the public by the Carlton Iron Co. and not the NER.

Trains on the Rosedale line were worked by various primitive systems as there was no signalling on the branch, although there was telegraphic communication (later telephone) between Battersby, Incline Top, Blakey, and the two Rosedale termini. In 1874 the time of opening for telegraphic purposes was 8-0 a.m. to 8-0 p.m. except at Rosedale East where there was a footnote, 'Time of closing uncertain, any time between 4-0 p.m. and 9-0 p.m.'. Ingleby Junction (Battersby) signalbox was open daily from 5-0 a.m. to 10-0 p.m. at that date.

The branch beyond the Incline Top was normally divided into three sections for operating purposes—Incline Top to Blakey Junction, Blakey to East Rosedale and Blakey to West Rosedale. In the 1892 Appendix to the Working Timetable, the West Rosedale to Blakey section was worked by Pilot Ring with one link; the East branch by a Pilot Ring with two links, and Blakey to Incline Top by a Pilot Ring with three links. Tickets were issued when there was more than one train on a section, these being red lettering on white for trains to the mines, and white lettering on black for trains from the mines. A signalman was stationed at Blakey to see that no engine travelled upon any of the three sections unless the driver had the proper ring in his possession for the section upon which he was to work. Engine drivers, *on pain of dis-*

missal, were not allowed to take a verbal order for entering a section. The 1898 Appendix lists only Staff & Ticket working on the branch, with no special instructions. By the time the 1911 Appendix was issued there were signs of economy on the branch and the man in charge of the staff arrangements at Blakey Junction was to be there only when more than one engine was working on the branch. The driver of the first engine to leave West Rosedale had to personally see the ring for the West Rosedale to Blakey Junction section and leave it for the following train, but he had to take with him the Incline Top and East Rosedale section rings and hand them over to the man in charge at Blakey, who then issued the rings as appropriate. The last train from Blakey Junction to West Rosedale carried the three sets of rings secured together by the man at Blakey Junction.

By March 1922, when the last NER Appendix was issued, the instructions in the table of "Single Lines over which Passenger Trains do not run" had not been amended and still referred to the "man at Blakey Junction." But by this time he

---

OUTPUT OF IRONSTONE AND DUST AT ROSEDALE 1910-1927

Year	Ironstone Tons	Calcined Dust Tons	Wayleave Payable for Ironstone £
1910	91,877	NIL	1,085
1911	65,910	NIL	1,014
1912	79,482	NIL	808
1913	146,738	NIL	772
1914	123,337	NIL	910
1915	93,310	NIL	814
1916	87,209	NIL	684
1917	92,479	154	666
1918	100,752	NIL	765
1919	74,295	NIL	706
1920	80,209	9,210	642
1921	25,826	25,546	639
1922	28,857	33,765	799
1923	19,312	39,855	262
1924	9,233	45,779	77
1925	14,749	28,387	123
1926	NIL	13,052	NIL
1927	NIL	35,910	NIL

had evidently been withdrawn because the additional regulations make no mention of him and the responsibility of obtaining the correct ring is placed upon the various drivers. To start with, the first driver away from the shed had to personally see the West Rosedale to Blakey Junction ring and leave it for the second driver. However, the first driver away had to take with him the ring for the section on which he was going to work, leaving the driver of the second train to carry the ring for the other section, together with the West Rosedale to Blakey ring, which had to be left in the staff cabin at Blakey. Whichever driver was first back at Blakey, on his way to the shed, had to leave his ring attached to the Blakey-West Rosedale ring in the staff cabin, in order that the driver of the second engine knew that he was the last one from Blakey Junction to West Rosedale. All the rings were then carried back to the shed on this engine. This method of working persisted until the instructions were deleted from the Appendix Supplement dated 31 July 1929.

On 12 November 1890 Driver Hudson, with engine 568, omitted to leave the pass rings at Blakey Junction when working a train to Incline Top. He decided to return to Blakey to leave the ring but on the way his train came into collision with engine 569 with Driver Jacob Baker. Each driver was fined five shillings. On 8 November 1892 Driver Hudson was fined 6s. 6d. for proceeding to Blakey for water instead of taking it at Heslets (Esklets), and colliding with a brakevan. Water was available at Esklets, near milepost 8 ($2\frac{1}{4}$ miles north of Blakey Junction), and at Sledshoe (Sledgeshoe) near milepost 11 ($\frac{3}{4}$ mile south of Blakey Junction) where a standard NER water crane was supplied from a reservoir on the hillside above. Tanks were also provided at the shed and on the East Rosedale branch one mile north of Blakey.

One of the worst difficulties on the line was snow, and at times the branch had to be closed for weeks on end until it could be cleared by snowploughs or men with shovels. During a snowstorm in 1867 a mineral train of nine wagons of ironstone was proceeding with an engine at front and rear when, in trying to get through some deep snow, the couplings parted between engine and tender of the leading locomotive. The engine leapt forward on its own, throwing Driver H. Turnbull and Fireman J. Aspinall off the footplate, but the engine was soon derailed and it turned end over end, finishing up some forty yards from the track. Five years later, by then a driver, Aspinall was driving a light engine on the branch when he came across a gang of platelayers with a rail out: the engine finished up down an embankment but the driver and fireman jumped clear at the last moment and were unhurt.

Because of the exposed position of this and other NER lines, the company built up a fleet of twenty-four large snow-ploughs between 1887 and 1909. Two of these were built in 1888 for the Rosedale branch and they were carried on four wheels, whereas all other NER ploughs were on six wheels. The two Rosedale ploughs, numbered 7 and 8, had a wheelbase of 9ft. 6in. and they were 21ft. 3in. long from the tip of the plough to the rear headstocks. The body of the plough had accommodation for the men and a cooking stove was fitted but when charging snowdrifts the men did not remain in the plough. This was partly because of the shock when the plough, propelled by two or three engines, met the wall of snow which it was hoped to move, and partly because if the plough became stuck in a deep drift it was impossible for the men to get out as the walls of snow blocked the doorways. These two ploughs appear to have been scrapped when the line was closed, but whether they were scrapped on site at West Rosedale, or taken down the incline for disposal, has not yet been discovered.

In 1917 the line was blocked for five weeks, from 8 January to 12 February. The drifts were ten to twenty feet in depth and in the cutting at Blakey the snow dug out had to be lifted some thirty feet to deposit it on top of the cuttings' sides. This could only be accomplished by passing the snow from man to man up the bank sides until the last man could dump it on the top of the pile! It took 75 men three days to clear this one cutting. Snow fell almost every day from 18 November 1916 to 18 April 1917, when four foot drifts were still appearing on the track.

Trains did not carry a tail lamp on the rear of the brake van but they did carry the usual two sidelights, which were to be lit in fog, falling snow, or during the hours of darkness. Passengers were not carried officially, although in June 1871 it was recommended that "a carriage with a proper brake be provided for the conveyance of Rosedale workmen between the mines and Ingleby Incline." The matter was referred to Mr. Fletcher but nothing is known of such a vehicle. Unofficially, passengers were conveyed in the brakevans but from January 1896 only employees and their families were allowed to travel in the vans and then for market day journeys only. This was brought about because it had been discovered that "several persons not connected with the railway, but residing at West Rosedale, East Rosedale, Blakey Junction, Incline

Top, and Incline Bottom were allowed to travel in the goods vans of the mineral trains between Blakey Junction and Rosedale Bank Top." One concession, allowed to Mr. Branfoot of The Lodge, Farndale, was that telegrams addressed to him could be transmitted over NER wires from Battersby to Blakey Junction at £1 1s. 0d. a year.

Some of the footplate crews seem to have preferred the rigours of life at Rosedale to that of the parent depot at Middlesbrough. Driver Jacob Baker, mentioned previously in connection with a collision, joined the NER at Rosedale as a cleaner on 1 August 1863, at a wage of 1s. 2d. per day: he was then just over 18 years of age, having been born on 11 June 1845. In 1870 he left the railway company's employment but he was re-engaged on 23 April 1873: he became a fireman on 8 November the same year. In June 1879 he moved to Gateshead, still as a fireman, at 4s. 0d. per day, but in November 1880 there was a vacancy for a driver at Rosedale and he moved back at 5s. 0d. per day. He then continued to serve as a driver at Rosedale for thirty-nine years and, in fact, until he retired on 7 February 1919 at the age of 73, having spent fifty-one years of his railway service at Rosedale. In addition to the collision between engines 568 and 569 mentioned previously, he was fined 5s. 0d. in September 1894 for "slow running with mineral train from Sherriff's Pit to Incline Top" on 23 August, and on 21 January 1899 he received a "strong caution" for 'knocking a wagon off the rails at Ingleby Incline Top' on 10 January. He died in September 1921.

Sherriff's Pit. Opposite: View of pit and buildings (R. Hayes). Above: Open shaft, as seen in 1966 with East Rosedale in the distance.

William Peirson joined the railway service as a fireman at Rosedale on 18 June 1883 at the age of twenty-one. On 2 November 1888 he "thoughtlessly left his work to speak to a Driver when the latter was shunting at Rosedale Incline Top, causing two trucks to leave the rails," and for this he was fined 2s. 0d. In 1889 he moved to Middlesbrough for four years but he returned to Rosedale, still as a fireman, in 1893: on 12 June 1899 he was promoted to driver but this meant moving to Newport and he didn't succeed in getting back to Rosedale until 1919, where he remained until his death in March 1927.

James Harker joined the NER on 22 November 1883 as "Fireman, Stationary Engine, Rosedale," at the age of fifteen. Seven years later he was appointed locomotive fireman and he spent three years on the footplate at Rosedale before moving to Carlin How in 1893, and later to Saltburn, Middlesbrough and West Hartlepool. On 28 February 1891 he was fined 3s. 6d. for "moving engine 580 during absence and without authority of driver, causing it to leave the rails at Blakey Junction" ten days previously.

Walter Mayman, who came from a well-known Rosedale

railway family, started his working life as a cleaner at Rosedale on 5 January 1891 at the age of fifteen. In 1896 he was promoted to fireman but at Newport, only to return to Rosedale in 1898. Still as a fireman he moved to Middlesbrough in 1903, Newport in 1904, Rosedale again in 1905, Newport in 1911, and Rosedale again on 22 September 1911. Promotion to driver from 1 January 1912 meant going to Newport again but in 1916 a fireman at Rosedale wished to move to the Middlesbrough area and Driver Mayman expressed a wish to go to Rosedale, even though it meant reverting to fireman and a drop in pay from 7s. 0d. to 5s. 0d. per day. After acting as spare driver at Rosedale he was reinstated as permanent driver on 1 April 1927, just in time to work the demolition train in the following year. On closure of the line he had once again to return to the Middlesbrough area and he retired from Newport shed in 1940. His son, who also started at Rosedale as a cleaner, retired a few years ago from British Railways as a running foreman at York shed.

Jeremiah Dawson was born in 1864 and started on the NER in 1880 as a cleaner at Middlesbrough. He was appointed fireman in 1882 but in 1895, due to colour blindness, he was transferred to Blakey Junction to receive and hand out the staffs and rings used to control working on the Rosedale branch. This full time post appears to have become redundant when he was transferred to Newport shed as fitters' assistant in December 1910, for the WTT Appendix for 1911 states that there would be a staff man in attendance at Blakey Junction "only when more than one engine is working on the branch and this will be arranged the previous day by the Locomotive Foreman."

The locomotive foreman at Rosedale in the 1890s was W. B. Thirkell, who retired in 1927 from a similar post at Starbeck after 51 years service with the North Eastern Railway. Then there was John Steward, born in 1854, who was transferred from Rosedale to Carlin How on 1 February 1902: he was followed by T. E. Duncan, formerly chief foreman at Middlesbrough Docks, who died in September 1906. His successor was G. H. Rothwell who stayed at Rosedale until 1 January 1912, when he was transferred to locomotive foreman at Kirkby Stephen. The NER records do not list any loco foreman at Rosedale after G. H. Rothwell and most probably, because of the decline in traffic, the shed was administered by a fitter-in-charge. For many years the district locomotive superintendent at Middlesbrough was L. Younghusband, who was also in overall charge of Saltburn, Carlin How and Battersby sheds.

In 1903 there were five engines and 18 men at Rosedale, and ten years later three engines and 12 men.

*   *   *

There was only one overbridge on the line, across the cutting at Blakey: this carried the Hutton-le-Hole to Castleton road but in the 1950s it was filled in and the road straightened. In the course of these improvements one parapet of the bridge was demolished but the other still stands on the left-hand side going north, just beyond the top of Blakey Bank. There was also only one level crossing on the main line, although a siding serving mines in Farndale crossed the road near the top of Blakey Bank. The level crossing at Blowith (also Blowath, Bloworth, or Blawith) crossed the rough moorland road known as Rudland Rigg.

Two cottages for men employed on the line were provided at Blowith Crossing and there were thirty-two other cottages:- Incline Foot 4; Incline Top 3; Blakey Junction 7; West Rosedale 16; and Black House ($3\frac{3}{4}$ miles from Blakey on the East branch) 2. Most have now disappeared but the row of cottages at West Rosedale still remains. In these houses many of the fittings were stamped with the letters N E R, including the water taps, and even the wooden lids of the coal fired coppers, in which the weekly wash was performed, were engraved with the same three letters.

Just on the Battersby side of the overbridge at Blakey a branch went off to the south, crossing the road up Blakey Bank and running parallel to the main road, but on the western side, for quarter of a mile. At the southern end of the branch there was a gantry above the line on which ran the tubs hauled up from mines in Farndale. These mines had a short life and worked only from 1873 to 1895. Signs of both the standard gauge branch and the narrow gauge incline down into Farndale can still be seen, together with the site of the engine house used to haul up the wagons.

Between Battersby and the foot of the Incline the line crossed the Kildale to Ingleby Greenhow road at Greenhow level crossing, and also a minor road leading to Ingleby Bank at Poultry House level crossing. The line then ran along the foot of the hills to the Incline Foot, climbing steadily at 1 in 50. Because of the gradient the loads of engines working trains from Battersby were restricted, and special braking instructions were in force for loaded trains from Incline Foot to Battersby.

SECTION	MAXIMUM LOAD IN TONS	
	Class 398 and Class 1001 0-6-0	Class P 0-6-0
Battersby Junction to Incline Foot	125	155
Incline Foot to Battersby Junction	435	545

On loaded trains running from Incline Foot to Battersby three single brakes for every four wagons had to be applied and it was the practice to leave one of the sidings empty at the junction so that if a train did get out of control the driver had a greater distance in which to stop his train.

At Battersby were numerous railway cottages and a three-road engine shed but the latter was demolished at the end of 1965. The shed was proposed in 1874, to hold eight engines, together with thirty cottages for the staff, and in May 1875 a tender of £2,500 1s. 4d. was accepted for the shed building and it was completed in 1877. The shed was closed after a few years, probably in 1879 with the failure of the Rosedale & Ferryhill Iron Co. Ltd., but it re-opened on 1 January 1889, only to close again on 30 November 1895, when there were four engines stationed there. After that the shed was used for a variety of purposes: in 1906 eight condemned engines were stored in the building awaiting sale or scrapping, and then in 1917 it accommodated six dining saloons made redundant because of the curtailment of refreshment facilities in World War I. In the 1920s the building was used as a miniature rifle range by the staff in the district, and in the 1930s it carried a large notice, TO LET. In World War II it was used as a store but then remained empty for many years before being demolished in 1965. A 42ft. turntable was provided adjacent to the shed. When Battersby shed was not open the traffic between Incline Foot and Battersby was worked by Stockton and Middlesbrough engines of Class 398, Class C, and Class P, all 0-6-0s.

Because of the difficulty in running round trains at Incline Foot it was the practice to propel the wagons on trains running from Battersby, with the engine leading on the return journey. An unusual visitor to this stretch of line in the 1920s was 2-2-4T 1679 on an officers' special from York: the driver and fireman took advantage of their trip and walked to the top of the Incline for a look round.

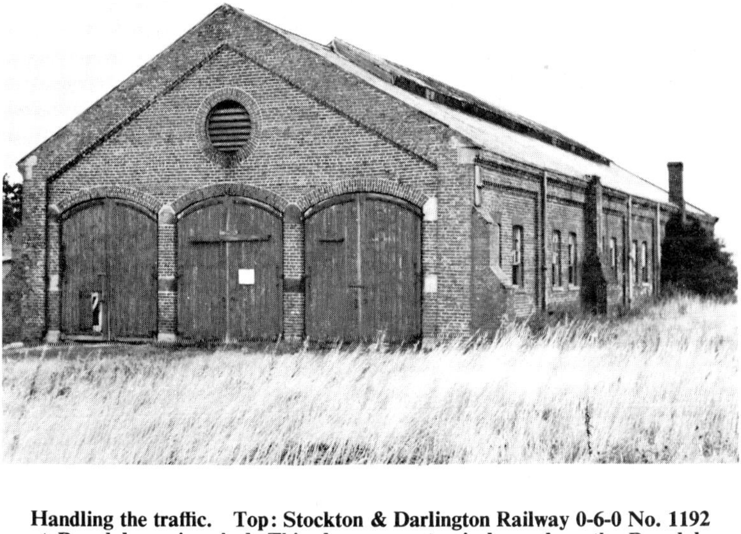

Handling the traffic. Top: Stockton & Darlington Railway 0-6-0 No. 1192 at Rosedale engine shed. This class was extensively used on the Rosedale branch between about 1900 and 1920 (photographer unknown). Bottom: Battersby engine shed, disused since 1895 for locomotive purposes. View taken in 1963 before the building was demolished.

Although never built, and although intended primarily for passenger traffic, the Lastingham & Rosedale Light Railway deserves mention, even though it approached Rosedale from the south and did not play any part in Cleveland railway history. In May 1899 an application to the Light Railway Commissioners was made by the Lastingham & Rosedale Estate Company for permission to build a standard gauge line just over eight miles long from Sinnington to Rosedale Abbey, where it was to terminate at Low Hollins. The line was to pass to the east of Appleton-le-Moors and Lastingham, and to the west of Hartoft, with a station for each village.

The Light Railway Order was granted on 31 July 1900 and the next move was an agreement with the NER for a junction with the latter's Pickering to Kirby Moorside branch. This agreement was signed on behalf of the Lastingham & Rosedale Railway & Estate Co. Ltd. and the Lastingham & Rosedale Light Railway Co., but the prospectus issued on 11 January 1902 was in the name of the Light Railway Co. only. Of the three directors, one lived at Wigan, one at Bolton, and one, Frederic Pope, at Lastingham. The prospectus also reveals that the company did intend to connect with the NER at Rosedale West "so as to forward goods and minerals to and from this Company's Railway to Middlesbrough and the North. The Directors believe that the line will ultimately be extended from Rosedale to the Whitby and Stockton line of the NER and so form another through route for passengers from the North to Scarborough, Malton, and the South."

The Light Railway Co. proposed to work the line with their own engines and servants, "believing that to be more economical than making a Working Agreement with another Company. Passenger traffic to be drawn from the resident and mining population, who, at Rosedale, are ten miles from a Railway Station, and from excursion traffic, which the Directors believe can be obtained from Scarborough, Whitby, Malton, York and Leeds, passengers coming for a whole or half day trip to Lastingham and the Moors." Quite an extensive freight traffic was also envisaged too, from the agricultural produce, timber, ironstone, flagstone, freestone, bricks, and possibly coal!

The authorised capital of the Light Railway Co. was £75,000, but the scheme was not successful financially and the *Railway Magazine* reported that £73,000 of the shares had been taken up by the contractors for the line and only £2,000 by the public. The light railway station was to have been on the north side of the NER line, on the opposite side of the

Marton road from the NER station, and extensive sidings were to have been provided for the exchange of the traffic which was expected. Although the first sod was cut near Rosedale Abbey on 14 June 1902 by Mrs. Muncaster, and the route actually staked out, the scheme faded away.

ROSEDALE BRANCH DISTANCES

	MILES	CHAINS	
BATTERSBY: zero post	00	00	
Battersby Junction	00	08	
Ayre's Siding	00	36	
Bank Bottom Siding	2	23	
Incline Bottom	2	53	
Incline Top	3	38	
Blowith Siding	4	33	Used by Earl of Feversham's tenants, Mr. Strickland, miller and others.
Blakey Junction	10	24	Siding used by Earl of Feversham's tenants (farmers). Farndale Siding used by Farndale Iron Co. (out of use 1895) 21ch. long.
Sherriff's Mine	12	07	Carlton Iron Co.
Rosedale Engine shed	13	76	
Bank Top Depot	14	20	Carlton Iron Co. Also West Rosedale Goods Siding used by General Public (wagon loads only).
West Branch terminus	14	27	
BLAKEY JUNCTION	00	00	
Nabscar Quarry Siding	2	61	Used by Mr. Richardson, stone merchant, from 1885 but out of use 1895.
East Rosedale Mines: (Junction to High Level sidings)	3	29	Carlton Iron Co.
East Rosedale Mines	3	74	Carlton Iron Co.
East Branch Goods Depot	4	48	

(NOTE: Although extracted from NER records the distances vary slightly according to which publication is used).

2: *Whitby to Loftus*

SANDSEND, to me, is not the same without the viaducts at East Row, at the foot of Lythe Bank, and at Newholm. Certainly the removal of the viaducts has opened up Sandsend but I always enjoyed seeing the coast line trains clanking slowly across these interesting structures.

The section of line between Whitby and Loftus was opened on 3 December 1883 by the Whitby, Redcar & Middlesbrough Union Railway, although the line was worked from the outset by the North Eastern Railway. The WR&MU company obtained their first Act of Parliament to build the line on 16 July 1866 but little was done and a further Act of 7 July 1873 was necessary to authorise the line as actually built from Bog Hall Junction at Whitby to Loftus. Even then the company was still in difficulty and after some work had been done on the line the company asked the NER to take it over and this was done under the Act of 19 July 1875.

The NER engineer was disgusted with the work that had already been carried out, with the bridges defective and the piers out of vertical, and some of the existing work had to be taken down and rebuilt because of its dangerous state. Even the surveys were so inaccurate that, had the original tunnels been completed, they were so out of line with each other that where boring was being done from each end they would not have met in the centre! Even the cast iron piers of the viaducts were filled with loose gravel instead of the concrete specified and a special machine had to be devised and built to force in liquid cement. Over £30,000 alone had to be spent on putting the viaducts in a proper state.

A tender for the completion of the line was awarded to the contractor John Waddell, who had submitted the figure of £146,163 12s. 0d., with completion date specified for 13 July 1881. However, such a large amount of extra work had to be done in rehabilitating the line that it was not ready until almost eighteen months later. When the WRMU directors complained about the delay they were politely told in no

Bird's eye views. Top: Scarborough—Middlesbrough train on the cliffs between Sandsend and Kettleness tunnels, about 1947 (Dr. Cobb). Bottom: Scenic excursion climbing up from Whitby Town to West Cliff, June 15th, 1958. The Whitby—Pickering line is in the top right-hand corner.

Larpool Viaduct. Opposite: Under construction (F. M. Sutcliffe). Right: The same viewpoint, September 4th, 1967.

uncertain terms that it was their own fault, and if they had ensured that the work was done properly in the first place then the delay would not have occurred. While the line was being completed the navvies employed on the job were proving a problem to adjoining landowners, and on 22 September 1879 the Easington Estate Company complained to the NER about the workmen trespassing on their land in search of game. They pointed out that the original company had agreed to pay the wages of a gamekeeper, and six days later the agent advised the NER that he had appointed a gamekeeper at 28s. 0d. a week. In March 1881 an account for this man's wages was submitted to the NER and this was followed up with a solici-

tor's letter requesting payment of the account, which the NER had still not paid by 18 January 1882. Unfortunately subsequent papers are missing and it is not known if the Estate Company ever did get their money.

On 17 February 1882 the Secretary of Trinity House wrote to the NER stating that the master of the brigantine *Colina* blamed the stranding of his ship on the fact that lights on the cliffs in the neighbourhood of Whitby had been mistaken for the Whitby lighthouse. Trinity House requested that the lights be screened and the NER replied immediately saying that they had asked the contractor that this should be done. The coastguards at Staithes and Whitby reported that it had been the practice to use open fires during the hours of darkness so that work on the railway could proceed, and that this had been going on for two or three years.

The work on the cliffs was mainly between Kettleness and Whitby, although the line was never very far from the sea: however, between Staithes and Loftus it did have to swing inland to get round the back of Boulby Cliff. The greatest activity was between Sandsend and Kettleness, where two tunnels had to be bored through projecting headlands: the longest was Sandsend tunnel, 1,652 yards long, which was a very uncomfortable tunnel to work through with steam locomotives. It closed in May 1958 when diesel multiple unit railcars were introduced between Scarborough and Middlesbrough via the Esk valley and Battersby. The shorter Kettleness tunnel, 308 yards long, was also built to replace the original course of the line round the face of the cliff: during the period when work was at a standstill this portion had fallen into the sea and the NER decided that the only safe way was to go through the two headlands. Going southwards from Kettleness station, along the trackbed of the now closed line, it is still possible to see the original course of the line where a shallow cutting goes off to the left, leading to the cliff edge.

There were two further viaducts on the line in addition to the three already mentioned: these were at Upgang (between Whitby and Sandsend) and at Staithes. The dimensions of the five viaducts were:-

VIADUCT	SPANS			
Upgang	5×60′	1×27′6″		
Newholm	9×30′	2×27′6″		
East Row	5×60′	1×57′6″	2×28′9″	
Sandsend	1×36′	5×30′	1×28′	1×27′6″
Staithes	6×60′	11×30′		

Staithes was, of course, the largest and most imposing of the five viaducts and it was 152ft. above the Roxby Beck. Because of the Tay Bridge disaster in December 1879, the Board of Trade issued instructions that all bridges should be designed to withstand a wind pressure of 56 lb. per sq. ft. Staithes viaduct, which had been completed in 1875 but not opened, had been designed to resist only 28 lb. sq. ft. To strengthen the structure extensive cross bracing was fitted and in addition a wind gauge was provided at the south end of the bridge. When the wind pressure reached 28 ft. per sq. ft. it caused a bell to ring in the signalbox and all traffic had to be

Scenes on the coast line. Top: Middlesbrough—Whitby train on Newholm Beck viaduct, between Sandsend and Whitby, about 1947 (Dr. Cobb). Bottom: Last train from Middlesbrough to Scarborough via Staithes at Kettleness, May 3rd, 1958, carrying the unofficial name, "The Economist."

stopped until the wind abated: once the bell had stopped ringing an inspection of the bridge had to be made by a platelayer before a train could be allowed to cross. Unfortunately the bell often rang when there was no wind blowing, and when there was a gale blowing it failed to ring! There is a story told of a driver who rang up the Staithes signalman from Easington (later Grinkle) to enquire if the bell was ringing: there was a gale blowing at the time but the bell was silent. When told this the driver said he was coming on and that he would not loiter on the viaduct. In fact he came across so fast that he could not stop the train in the station and had to reverse back. The bridges were all demolished in 1960 after the line had closed to traffic. The last through trains were the 4-20 p.m. from Middlesbrough to Scarborough, with engine 80116 carrying the headboard "The Economist" to show why the line was being closed, and the 4-24 p.m. from Scarborough to Middlesbrough with engine 67754.

North of Staithes the line skirted the back of Boulby Cliff, passing the site of sidings for the ironstone mines at Grinkle Park: the latter were served from 1917 by an incline up which wagons were hauled from the picturesque valley where the mines were situated. There were also sidings serving the Boulby mines, reached along an embankment and then a tunnel under the main road. This area is now dominated by the headshaft of the potash mine which is being sunk by I.C.I. Ltd.

To reach Easington (renamed Grinkle from 1 April 1904) the line had to pass through a third tunnel, 993 yards long, and the section from Boulby, through the tunnel to Loftus and Carlin How, will have to be reinstated if traffic from the potash mine is to be conveyed by rail as proposed. At the north end of the tunnel a few grassy mounds indicate the site of Grinkle station, which had the usual station buildings—booking office, waiting rooms, signalbox, goods shed, etc., together with a house for the stationmaster, but now all swept away. The station closed temporarily on 11 September 1939 because of World War II, but it never did reopen and although freight trains may once more rattle through the tunnel they will not stop at the station and the ghosts of long dead passengers and staff can remain undisturbed.

There was no formal opening ceremony of the WRMU on 3 December 1883, but before the first train was due to start a large number of people assembled in Whitby station and there was a general rush to obtain the first tickets for the different stations on the line. So great was the number of passengers that additional carriages had to be attached to the train and, although this delayed the starting, many passengers were allowed to proceed without tickets. Cheers were raised as the train started and bunting was freely displayed. Mr. Edward Corner, J.P., the chairman of the original company, and a "select party of friends" left by the 9-55 a.m. train for Middlesbrough, where they adjourned to the Cleveland Club: "here Mr. Corner entertained his friends to an impromptu champagne luncheon in honour of the occasion." At Hinderwell there was a large crowd, with a band, and an address of congratulations was presented to Mr. Corner.

"Notwithstanding the crush and circumstances of everything being new, not the slightest hitch of any kind occurred—if we accept that some of the trains were a little late—a circumstance not unusual on the oldest and best lines. All agree that the new line is not only one of the most picturesque, but also the smoothest and easiest they ever travelled upon." Whitby station sold 479 tickets on the first day and West Cliff 352. The first sod had been cut near Sandsend in May 1871 by the Dowager Marchioness of Normanby, "the progress of the undertaking to completion having been retarded by natural obstacles and engineering difficulties which, at one time, threatened to be almost insuperable but which have at last been surmounted only with the most dauntless energy and perseverance."

The original company ran into financial difficulty largely because of the natural difficulties which were encountered and which had not been anticipated. The trouble on the cliffs near Kettleness, the landslips at Easington and other places, ate up the money and work came to a standstill. The original contractor was John Dickson and in 1874, when work had stopped, two 0-6-0ST locomotives were advertised for sale. These were named *Penwyllt* and *Mulgrave* and they were valued at £775 and £875 respectively, with *Penwyllt* stated as being in a very bad state of repair, and *Mulgrave* as having done little if any work. They were considered by the Consett Water Co. but turned down, and *Mulgrave* was purchased in September 1874 by Thomas B. Nelson of York for £750. On 24 September, Nelson's men started to remove *Mulgrave* from the cliffs, where she stood, and the engine arrived at York three days later. After Nelson had sent off his cheque for £750 he found that the engine was not in as good condition as he expected and in later correspondence it is stated that "Nelson is very sore about his purchase of the *Mulgrave*." C. Morrison, whose address is given as Gresham Street,

Eighty years of "progress." Opposite page, top: Sandsend station under construction, about 1880 (F. M. Sutcliffe). Opposite page, bottom: Demolition of Sandsend viaduct, October 13th, 1960. This page: Demolition of Staithes viaduct, April 6th, 1960 (British Railways).

London, offered £650 for *Penwyllt* but the company wanted £700; after three weeks Morrison dropped his offer to £600, and as Nelson was only offering £500, they decided to accept Morrison's offer. However, even he was unhappy about his purchase and in July 1875 he wrote to the WRMU and complained about the state of the engine, which he had repaired and resold. He also pointed out a discrepancy in the builders' plate carried by the engine: he already owned Fox, Walker No. 127, built in 1872; whereas *Penwyllt* carried a plate with No. 29 and the date 1873! No doubt Morrison was also sore about the deal, especially as it cost him £335 4s. 10d. to repair the engine, including £200 for a new firebox. Fortunately some details of engines working the line in its early days have survived and the following notes have been extracted from traffic books maintained at Carlin How:-

Whitby goods:—Class 398:3 (later renumbered 1451), 17, 195,204,626,641,1133,1370.
Class 59:682.

Whitby passengers:—Class A 537; Class BTP 63; Class 38 112; Class 59: 508,812,1141; Class 1265 1270.

Whitby excursions:—Class BTP 43,173,321; Class 38: 158; Class 59: 232, 440; Class 398: 170, 204,236,475,617,626,682,1119,1380 (on trains from Guisborough, Stockton, Middlesbrough, Newcastle, Birtley, Shildon, Stanhope, etc.)

Officers' Specials, Stores Vans etc:—Class 59: 508; Class 398 236; Class 447 449; Class 1463 1466/9/72.

The above is just a sample of the engines noted in 1884 and 1885.

By 1906 most of the passenger traffic was worked by three types of tank engines—Class BTP, Class A and Class O, with Class 398 and Class 1001 0–6–0 on the goods. Engines noted were:—

Class BTP:-87,91,466,591.
Class A:205, 469, 537,1577/83/97.
Class O:381/94,427/35/6,505/26/40/80,1331/4,1703/39/95, 1888/9, 1914,2081/91.
Class 398:90,170,339,616,1038,1119,1426.
Class 1001:1030/40/6,1221/77.

Changing the single line tablets at Prospect Hill signalbox, Whitby (photographer unknown).

Other engines noted were: Class B 503; Class C 289; Class P 1899,1944/5/6/8/57/60; Class P1 463,1714,2034/5/41,2133/5/6; Class 38: 1331; Class 59: 192,446,508; Class 93: 512,645,659; Class 957:957; Class 1238:1240.

The Class A 2–4–2T and the Class O 0–4–4T continued to work the passenger trains well into LNER days and, in fact, the Class O engines still worked the line occasionally in British Railways' days. The Class W 4–6–0T (later rebuilt as 4–6–2T) worked from Saltburn, Whitby and Scarborough sheds but the engines which put in the most slogging work were the A5 and A8 4–6–2Ts, helped out towards the end by V1/V3 2–6–2Ts and L1 2–6–4Ts. During the summer months tender engines often appeared and in the mid-1930s the most common class was the J39 0–6–0, normally not allowed because of size and weight but passed for the line when traffic grew so rapidly after the change of northern terminus from Saltburn to Middlesbrough. However, a nasty derailment of one of this class near Prospect Hill, Whitby, put an end to their work on this line. In the 1950s Class B1 4–6–0s and LMS 4MT 2–6–0s did a lot of work. The goods traffic was worked by the P1 (LNER J25) 0–6–0s until the end of the line in 1958, Until March 1936 no instructions were issued regarding the engines allowed to work between Whitby West Cliff and Loftus, but in that year the first restriction was issued, covering only Class V1. At the end of the same year Classes B16, K3 and V2 were also barred. On 1 September 1939 a more comprehensive list was issued, restricting Classes A1,A3,A4,B16,J28,J35,J39,K3,N8,N10,04, P2, Q5,Q6,Q7,V1 and V2.

Under the later Route Availability scheme introduced just after the end of World War II the West Cliff-Loftus section was classed as RA4, which allowed such classes as G5,A6, 4MT: in addition engines of higher RA class were permitted, such as A5,A8,B1,D20,D49,L1,Q6,V1 and V3.

3: *Loftus to Middlesbrough*

THE route beyond Loftus to Middlesbrough has a complicated history. Basically it was built by two companies, the Cleveland Railway and the Middlesbrough & Guisborough Railway, although the final section of the Cleveland, across the Kilton valley from Carlin How to Loftus, was actually completed by the North Eastern Railway. The Cleveland Railway was planned to run from the Tees, southwards and eastwards, into the rapidly developing ironstone district of Cleveland, to tap the supplies of ore for use in the ironworks at Port Clarence. An Act of Parliament for the Guisborough-Loftus section was obtained in July 1858, and for the Guisborough to river Tees portion in July 1861. However, as most of the latter had been constructed under wayleaves and was almost complete at the time of the Act, it was possible to open from east of Guisborough to the Tees on 23 November 1861. The line was extended eastwards to Boosbeck in 1862, on to Brotton in 1865, and finally across Kilton Viaduct in 1867.

In 1863 the NER absorbed the Stockton & Darlington Railway (which had taken over the Middlesbrough & Guisborough Railway in 1858) and in 1865 the Cleveland Railway, thus coming into possession of two routes from Tees-side to Guisborough. Previously the NER chairman had been lamenting that his company had not got a finger in the Cleveland ironstone pie! It was soon decided that the Middlesbrough & Guisborough line via Nunthorpe would be the better of the two routes and that by putting in a short connecting link to the Cleveland line at Guisborough a route could be provided from Middlesbrough to Loftus, serving many of the ironstone mines on the way. Thus the Cleveland line was closed and abandoned between Flatts Lane (Ormesby) and Guisborough, but the embankment on which it ran can still be seen on the north side of the Ormesby-Guisborough road (A171). Nearer Guisborough, as it approached the town from the north-west, the line originally ran on a wooden viaduct on Admiral Chaloner's land, but after standing out of use for some time the viaduct was blown down in a gale in 1881 and the whole structure was removed.

The Cleveland Railway skirted the south-west side of the town and crossed the Middlesbrough & Guisborough line on an overbridge just outside the latter company's station. It was in this area that the connecting line between the two was built, leaving the M&G line at what was known as Hutton Junction, or Guisborough Junction. As a result Guisborough station, which was a terminus, was left at the end of a short spur and a complicated operation had to be carried out by passenger trains between Middlesbrough and Brotton which had to call at Guisborough. If travelling from Middlesbrough the train ran into the station in the normal way and then, when station duties had been completed, the engine backed out its train to the junction. Once over the points the train reversed direction again and headed for Brotton. In the opposite direction a train from Brotton ran past the junction, backed its train into the station, and then reversed again and set off for Middlesbrough. This method of working persisted after the steam trains were withdrawn on 5 May 1958 and, in fact, until the Loftus-Middlesbrough service ceased on 2 May 1960. A Middlesbrough-Guisborough service survived until 2 March 1964 but now the station site has been cleared and the attractive small station, with its overall roof and unusual glass end panels, has disappeared in the march of progress.

Slapewath, just east of Guisborough, was an important point on the railway, both in the early years under the Cleveland Railway ownership, and later under North Eastern control, and it was the centre of a number of branches to ironstone mines. One of the longest branches eventually ran two miles northwards to serve Park Pit, adjacent to the Guisborough-Skelton road. Other branches ran from Slapewath to Slapewath Mines (passing under the Guisborough-Whitby road), Spawood Mines, Stanghow Mines, and Aysdalegate Mines (in the angle of the road at the foot of Birk Brow, again on the Whitby road). The bridge carrying the Park Pit branch over the Whitby road was demolished some years ago during road improvements, but the narrow bridge over the Cleveland main line is still used by today's road traffic, which is particularly heavy during the summer months with people from Teesside and South-east Durham bound for Whitby and Scarborough. Further mines were at Boosbeck, Lumpsey, Brotton, and on Hunt Cliff, the headland south of Saltburn around which the railway ran to serve the mines, rather than strike across the unproductive neck of land between Brotton and Carlin How. Yet more mines were to be found at Skinningrove, Loftus (actually in the bed of the Kilton valley and served by the zig-zag line), and at Liverton (at the south end of Kilton viaduct).

Skinningrove ironworks were established in 1873 and present a striking, if dirty picture perched on the cliff above the small harbour. At one time a railway incline ran from inside the works to the harbour but this line has now been abandoned. The lines on the harbour were worked by an unusual vertical boiler locomotive built by Cochrane & Co. of Middlesbrough in 1871 known as "Coffee-Pot": it survived until the 1950s.

To reach Liverton Mines and the terminus at Loftus a large viaduct had to be built across the Kilton valley. It consisted of stone piers with iron girders: it had twelve spans of 45 ft., and one of 52ft. to accommodate the reversing neck of the zig-zag line to the floor of the valley below. In fact at its highest point the viaduct was 150ft. above the Kilton Beck. It was built on a curve of 18 chains radius. The foundations were gradually undermined by ironstone workings: in 1911 passenger traffic had to be stopped because of the condition of the viaduct, and it was decided to convert it into an embankment by burying it in refuse from the numerous local mines. Altogether some 720,000 tons of spoil were required and the task was completed in 1913. While trains were barred from the viaduct, passengers were conveyed between Loftus and Skinningrove stations by motor char-a-banc, and the ironstone from Liverton Mines had to be carried to Middlesbrough by way of Whitby and Battersby. To allow the Kilton Beck to continue to flow down the valley to the sea, a massive reinforced concrete culvert had to be built before tipping commenced. The NER agreed to purchase the strip of land under the culvert so that it was not disturbed by mine workings. Formerly the land under the viaduct had been reserved by the NER but this was given up when the embankment was completed. This section is another portion of line which will have to be rehabilitated for the railway to be relaid from Carlin How to reach the ICI potash mine at Boulby.

To reach Loftus mines and Skinningrove gasworks a zig-zag line was built from Carlin How, down the side of the valley, with a reversing neck under the northernmost span of the viaduct. This first leg was 55 chains long, with a reversing neck of 9 chains, followed by the second leg 59 chains long, and another reversing neck at the seaward end of the line to allow trains to run along the floor of the valley to the gasworks and mines sidings. As might be expected the gradients were severe:

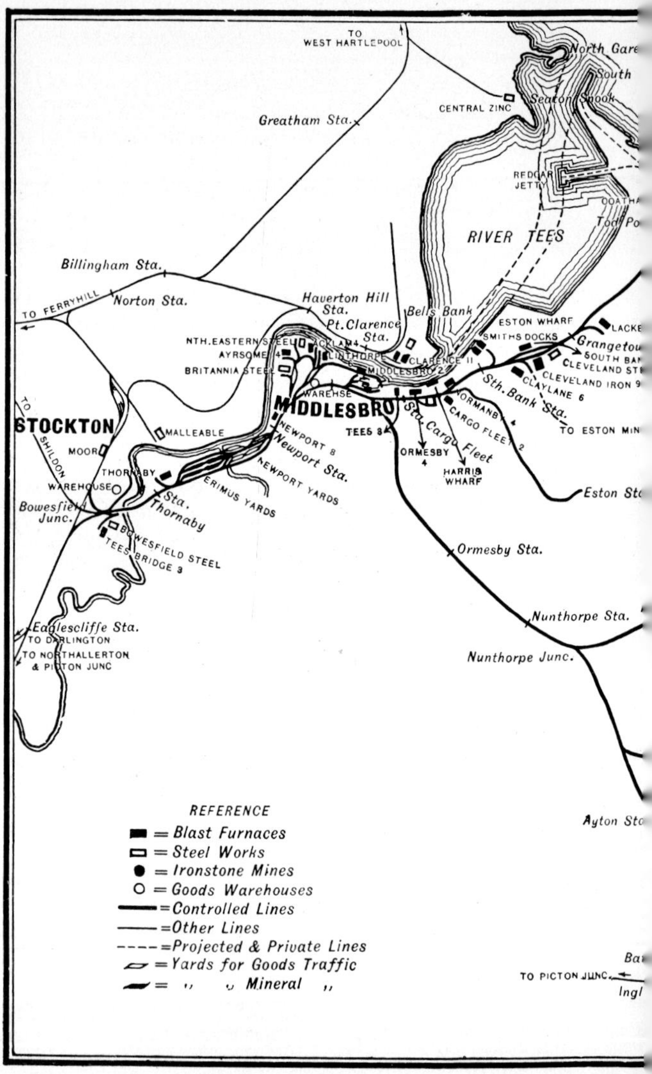

The numerals next to blast furnaces indicate the number of furnaces

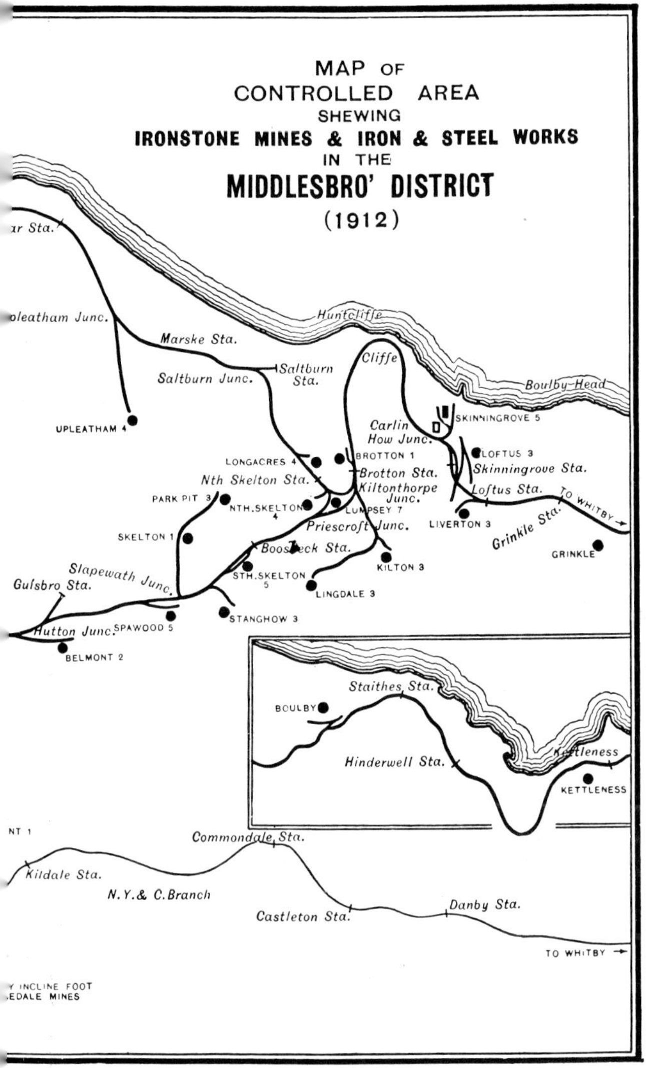

to ironstone mines, the number of trains of stone despatched daily.

leaving Carlin How the line at first descended at 1 in 74 but this soon steepened to 1 in 37: the whole of the second leg was at 1 in 28! Loads were, of course, severely restricted and one engine was allowed to take only 7 loaded wagons, two engines 15 loaded wagons, and three engines 22 loaded wagons. Leaving the bottom reversing neck it was the practice to have the two assisting engines leading, with the train engine on the rear: thus after reversing under the viaduct and slogging up the last bank the assisting engines were in the rear and they could drop off as soon as the train engine had control of the load. Mr. W. Huby, who was stationmaster at Skinningrove from 1934 to 1937, recalls that his father was also stationmaster there between 1883 and 1896, and in this period (about 1892) his brother was responsible for averting what might have been a serious accident. As a 15 wagon train was leaving the viaduct reversing neck with an engine at each end, the leading engine and half the train took the correct road, but the points failed under the middle of the train and the rear half and the banking engine took the descending line. As the banking engine was not coupled to the rear wagons it could not hold them and there was a distinct possibility that the wagons would run amain down the bank and end up in a tangled mass at the end of the second reversing neck. Fortunately the episode was seen, and the danger appreciated, by Mr. Huby's brother who was fireman on the leading engine. He jumped off his engine, ran down the bank separating the two legs of the incline, and intercepted the wagons before they were going too fast to jump aboard. Fortunately they were of the usual end-braked type and by walking along the top of the wagons he was able to apply sufficient brakes to bring them to a stand.

On another occasion Mr. Huby (senior) was on Skinningrove station when he saw the Whitby goods blithely descending the first leg of the zig-zag instead of running on its correct line through the station. Fortunately he was able to attract the crew's attention and they managed to stop the train before it hit the buffers at the end of the first reversing neck. The most tragic occurrence was in 1880, when the former Stockton & Darlington 0–6–0 1220 ran out of control while descending with 14 loaded and 8 empty wagons. On the footplate at the time, in addition to the driver and fireman, were a youth who had brought the driver's tea and a locomotive inspector with his son and a friend. After colliding with the buffers at the end of one of the reversing necks the engine ran tender-first up the bank and came to rest with the tender tilted up: the son of the locomotive inspector was trapped by the tender and before he could be freed he was scalded to death by steam from a broken gauge-glass.

In 1866 four 0–6–0ST engines were delivered from Robert Stephenson & Co. for work on the zig-zag line but they were not entirely successful and after a few years' work they were rebuilt as 0–6–0 tender engines: they originally carried the names *Roseberry, Kildale, Whitby,* and *Escomb*, and the numbers 196–9 respectively. They were followed in 1876 by four more engines built especially for the line, this time as 0–6–0Ts carrying numbers 1037, and 1292–4: they were later known on the NER as Class 1037, and they continued to work the line until scrapped after a life of about 35 years. Following the demise of the Stockton & Darlington 0–6–0s and the Class 1037 tanks, the newer Class P 0–6–0 appeared and until closure in 1958 the only engines allowed on the zig-zag were the four varieties of 4′ 7¼″ mineral 0–6–0s of classes P, P1, P2 and P3, together with the Class C 0–6–0 with 6″ larger wheels.

On the west side of the Kilton valley, about 1½ miles up from the viaduct, were Kilton Mines, established in 1870 and served by a privately built branch railway opened on 11 June 1873, which joined the NER at Kilton Junction, ¾ mile south of Brotton. This line was taken over by the NER in the following year, and later a branch was built by Pease & Partners from the Kilton Mines branch to their Lingdale Mines. The Kilton branch closed in 1963 when the mines ceased production: Lingdale Mines had closed the previous year.

The last ironstone mine in Cleveland was the North Skelton mine, which closed on 17 January 1964. This was situated on the North Skelton-Priestcroft Junction loop, which formed part of a triangular layout of tracks. The other two sides of the triangle were the Boosbeck-Brotton line of the Cleveland Railway, and the Saltburn-Brotton line (the Saltburn Extension). The Priestcroft loop and the Saltburn Extension were authorised under the NER and Cleveland Railway Act of 5 July 1865, by which the NER was empowered to take over the Cleveland Railway and to build various branches and connections to complete the Cleveland picture.

The Saltburn Extension line originally had no stations but North Skelton was opened in 1902: the line was opened to mineral and goods traffic on 1 July 1872 and to passenger traffic on 1 April 1875. Its main purpose was to provide a direct route from the Brotton/Loftus area to the numerous works east of Middlesbrough without going round via Slapewath and Nunthorpe, which also necessitated a reversal at Middlesbrough. The scope of the Extension line was widened when in 1878 the Priestcroft loop was opened: this then allowed trains from the Boosbeck and Slapewath areas to reach the works and blast furnaces east of Middlesbrough, again without reversal.

The passenger services in the area were complicated by the number of reversals necessary at intermediate stations. For instance, Saltburn-Whitby-Scarborough trains had to reverse first at Saltburn West to join the line through North Skelton to Brotton, Loftus and the south, and a Saltburn-Guisborough service reversed again at Brotton to reach Guisborough, where yet a third reversal was required to gain the station. Until 1917 there was a service via the Priestcroft loop but from 1 October 1917 the sole remaining train was diverted via Brotton and had to reverse like the others. However, these services were developed from 1905 when the NER autocars were introduced. These units consisted of a small tank locomotive with one or two coaches, and in the latter case the engine was placed between the coaches. The train could be driven from the outer end of each coach, with only the fireman on the engine to look after the fire and the boiler. Thus, when the train required to reverse it was only necessary for the driver to walk from one end to the other: there was no need for the engine to be uncoupled and run round the coaches before coupling on again at the opposite end, as was necessary with ordinary coaches. As these units were withdrawn they were replaced in the 1920s by Sentinel steam railcars—a coach with a self-contained boiler and cylinders, which could also be driven from either end. These Sentinel cars were all named after stage coaches of earlier days and they lasted until the 1940s. Later larger Sentinel cars with twelve cylinders were provided for working through to Whitby and Scarborough and one was usually stationed at Guisborough. These were also named after stage coaches and carried the names *Old John Bull, Old Blue, Defence, Royal Sovereign, and Tantivy*. They disappeared from the scene in the early 1940s and their place was taken by normal steam trains, some of which operated on the push-and-pull principle, similar to the NER autocars mentioned above.

Although the new British Railways diesel railcars had been used on some services in the area, it was on 5 May 1958 that a general change over to these vehicles was made. On this date the service south of Loftus was withdrawn and the section as far as Whitby West Cliff closed completely. The Loftus-Middlesbrough service was cut back to Guisborough in May 1960 and the Guisborough service ceased in March 1964,

Brotton station. Top: The exterior in 1908 (photographer unknown). Bottom: View in 1959 showing freight train from Skinningrove ironworks (T. E. Rounthwaite).

bringing to an end passenger services in the area, although the Middlesbrough-Redcar-Saltburn line continued in use, as did the Middlesbrough-Great Ayton-Battersby-Whitby service.

Until 1932 the service along the coast was provided between Saltburn and Scarborough, but from 1933 it was altered to run between Middlesbrough and Scarborough. Due to the larger population which could easily avail themselves of the new facilities, and with the popularity of Holiday Runabout Tickets, the passenger traffic increased in leaps and bounds, only to be brought to a stop by the wartime restrictions. However, after 1945 the service developed again until on some days the line, because of its single-line sections, was carrying as many trains as possible.

However, as mentioned earlier, the section between Loftus and West Cliff was closed from 5 May 1958 and henceforward Middlesbrough-Scarborough trains were routed via Battersby (reverse), Whitby Town (reverse), West Cliff (reverse), and a further reversal was necessary to enter Scarborough station. The next move was to close West Cliff station (from 12 June 1961) and trains then reversed at Prospect Hill Junction, where the line from Whitby Town climbed up to join the Scarborough line. Finally the section from Whitby to Scarborough, through Robin Hoods Bay and Ravenscar, was closed on 8 March 1965.

The local service between Saltburn and Brotton ceased in 1951 but in the summer months up to and including 1957

Station architecture. Opposite: Hutton Gate station as converted to a private residence, June 1st, 1970. Above: Pinchinthorpe old station, August 10th, 1964.

some of the Scarborough-Middlesbrough trains ran via the Saltburn Extension to provide a service to Marske, Redcar, Grangetown, South Bank etc. without the passengers having to go into Middlesbrough and change trains. This line is still open for freight traffic to Skinningrove Ironworks and it is, of course, eventually to be reopened to Boulby. Between Saltburn and North Skelton is the handsome brick viaduct across the Skelton Beck, with 11 arches and totalling 783 ft. in length. The line, originally double track, is now single.

It is now necessary to return to the Guisborough area and the Middlesbrough & Guisborough Railway, which was opened to goods traffic on 11 November 1853, and to passenger traffic on 25 February 1854. The earliest ironstone mines served were those at Cod Hill, some two miles south-west of Guisborough, owned by Pease & Co. and opened in 1855. A branch to the mines diverged from the M&G line about half a mile west of Hutton Gate station, skirted the parkland surrounding Hutton Hall, and climbed up to Hutton Moor. Much of the course of the line can still be seen by taking the road which passes under the railway (although the bridge spanning the road has now been removed) to the west of

Hutton Gate station, and then across Hutton Park to Hutton Lowcross, where houses have recently been built on the bed of the line, which closed about 1865 after a life of only ten years. Until 1 October 1903 Hutton Gate station was used solely by the Pease family from nearby Hutton Hall, but after the collapse of Messrs. J. & J. W. Pease's bank the station was closed. However, it re-opened as a public station on 1 January 1904: it finally closed on 2 March 1964. Since then it has been sold by British Railways and converted into an attractive private residence.

The engine shed at Carlin How appears to have been opened in 1866, when a tender of £1,261 13s. 0d. was received for a shed and an unspecified number of cottages. In 1873 it was suggested that the engine shed should be converted to a goods shed and the engines transferred to Middlesbrough, but in 1875 it was proposed that the shed should be lengthened to take four additional engines. To accomplish this it was decided to use a redundant wooden shed from Shildon, and to place it at the west end of the existing shed, but in the following year a new wooden shed and a number of cottages were suggested "as they would be less liable to damage or subsidence." Plans for the shed and the cottages were submitted and approved in 1877 and expenditure of £9,500 authorised. Further extensions and alterations amounting to £1,000 were carried out in 1893. In 1895 the following engines were stationed at Carlin How:-

Class 1001 0-6-0: 1004/13/28/49, 1109/26/8/48/67, 1220.
Class 1037 0-6-0T: 1037, 1292/4.
Class BTP 0-4-4T: 1115.

By 1892/3 the following engines and crews were at Carlin How:-

Class 1001:
1004 Driver Lancaster — 1028 Driver G. Warrior
1046 Driver Moore — 1049 Driver R. Glover
1148 Driver G. Glover — 1201 Driver M. Glover
1220 Driver Morris

Class 1037:
1037 Driver Thomas — 1292 Driver R. Glover (from 1049)

Class BTP:
1115 ? (when this engine was stopped for washout or repair, 63, 189 or 1058 was borrowed from Middlesbrough).

On 31 July 1902 the NER General Manager suggested that owing to the closing of Liverton Mines, and the consequent reduction in work, the shed should be closed and the engines and men transferred as follows:-

1 engine and 2 sets of men to Saltburn
2 ,, 2 ,, Haverton Hill
6 ,, 6 ,, Middlesbrough

Consequently the shed was closed from 31 October 1902 and by 1906 it held seven condemned engines awaiting sale or scrapping: this is undoubtedly the shed referred to by E. L. Ahrons in his closing lines of the NER section of *Locomotive and Train Working in The Latter Part of the Nineteenth Century,* where he describes a deserted shed "somewhere on the north east coast" in which were stored a number of old engines. Ahrons refers to some thirty engines but there was no closed North Eastern shed where so many engines could be stored and he could only have been writing about Carlin How.

The BTP 0–4–4T engine at Carlin How, 1115, replaced the Stockton & Darlington Railway 2–4–0 of 1856 with the same number (originally 115 *Meynell*) on the passenger services. The shed reopened early in 1907 and continued in use until 1921 but the building remained standing until 1954 or 1955: the site can still be located by the filled in inspection pits. Now the trains to Skinningrove ironworks are hauled by diesel locomotives and the steam engine has disappeared from BR metals. The works themselves have also gone over to diesels and the interesting steam shunters have gone but fortunately most of them—in particular *Minnie,* built in 1878, have been recorded on film.

4: The Esk Valley

MENTION has been made in the Rosedale chapter of the North Yorkshire & Cleveland Railway, which commenced at Picton on the Northallerton to Stockton line, and pushed eastwards towards Grosmont and a connection with the Whitby & Pickering Railway. For most of its length the NY&C served only rural and agricultural needs, but from Potto a branch went off to the south, through Swainby, to serve ironstone mines at Whorlton on land owned by the Duke of Aylesbury: these mines were variously known as Swainby, Whorlton, or Aylesbury mines.

The section from Picton to Stokesley was opened to the public on 3 March 1857, together with the Whorlton branch, 2 miles 6 chains, and within a short time there were two trains of ironstone per day on to the NY&C main line at Potto, and thence via Picton and the former Leeds Northern line to Stockton. Traffic ceased in 1892 and the rails were lifted in 1904: a North Eastern gate protecting a long vanished level crossing in the centre of Swainby was still in place in the 1960s —and may still be there to this day.

The line from Stokesley gradually extended westwards until it reached Castleton on 1 April 1861, by which time the NY&C had been taken over by the NER. At some date unknown, but certainly in the nineteenth century, a branch was built from Commondale station to serve a brick and tileworks in Commondale village. This line, $\frac{5}{8}$ mile long, was owned by the brick company and was not a NER branch: it was worked latterly by the brick company's Barclay 0–4–0ST of 1872 carrying the name *Lascelles,* which after some years' inactivity was cut up in 1955. The red bricks produced by the local works were used for building a number of houses in the neighbourhood and they look strange in this country of stone walls and stone houses.

The final section of the NY&C from Castleton to Grosmont was not opened until 2 October 1865 and at last it was possible to run a service the whole length of the Esk Valley, using the

Whitby & Pickering between Grosmont and Whitby. There were four passenger trains in each direction, at 7–45 am, 10-40 am, 3–30 pm and 8–40 pm. from Stockton, and 7–15 am, 10–30 am, 3–15 pm and 6–15 pm from Whitby, stopping at all stations and taking between 2 hours 5 minutes and 2 hours 14 minutes. Empty ironstone wagons ran at 6–0am. Stockton to Ingleby; 6–0 am, 8–0 am and 1–0 pm Darlington to Ingleby (ex Ferryhill); and at 8–30 am and 1–0 pm from Stockton to Potto, with a coke train to Grosmont entering the branch at Picton at 2–30 pm. Unfortunately the Working Timetable does not show the origin of this train but it may have been the 12–25 pm from Waterhouses via Leamside, where a reversal was necessary: it was booked for two engines if required.

In the opposite direction there were loaded ironstone trains from Ingleby to Ferryhill at 10–45 am, 11–40 am and 4–35 pm, while the 4–50 pm from Ingleby ran only as far as Stockton. There were two similar trains from Potto at 11–10 am and 3–0 pm. The engine(s) working the Grosmont coke train returned with the empties at 6–45 pm from Grosmont. There was an ordinary goods at 8–0 am from Stockton, returning from Whitby at 2–30 pm, although if running late on the outward journey it turned round at Grosmont: in this event Whitby turned out an engine to work the westbound traffic as far as Grosmont and the engine returned with the traffic off the goods.

The coke for Grosmont was for use in the ironworks established there in 1862 by C. & T. Bagnall: at first two blast furnaces were in operation and a third was blown in in 1875, by which time there were two trains of coke and coal per day to feed the works, running from the Stockton & Darlington section via Allens curve, near Eaglescliffe. The ironstone was mined from the hillsides adjacent to the ironworks and, in fact, at a later stage there was sufficient stone to supply other ironworks. However, due to the competition from the works on Tees-side the ironworks at Grosmont closed down in 1891 and the equipment was sold. The works were bought by Messrs. A. Gladstone who, according to NER records, took over Bagnall's sidings. At a later date (1903) Wm. Schofield & Son commenced to remove the slag heaps. J. & J. Dunwell and their successors continued to operate the adjacent brickworks until the late 1950s. Little is known of the locomotives used at the ironworks but there were probably four 0–4–0Ts, of which one had a vertical boiler: one of the normal locomotives carried the name *Arncliffe* and this had come from Glaisdale Ironworks when they were sold up in 1888.

Train in sylvan surroundings at Glaisdale (photographer unknown).

The Glaisdale Ironworks were established in 1864 and production commenced in 1866. These works changed hands a number of times and the final owners were the South Cleveland Iron Co. There were three blast furnaces but after an operative life of only ten years production ceased in 1876. The works then stood out of use for some years until sold by auction on 11 July 1888, when they were purchased by John Dickson of Sandsend, who was probably the same contractor who built the first portion of the Whitby, Redcar & Middlesbrough Union Railway in 1873/4. North Eastern Railway records show that he used his own engine during the time the works were being dismantled and the late George Harland of Glaisdale states that this engine carried the name *Busy Bee,* which was probably one of the locomotives used when the works were in operation. Again, little is known of the works engines. Mr. Dickson was still dismantling the works in 1895 and at a later date the slag heaps were sold to the Surrey County Council: the Council rented the former South Cleveland Iron Company's siding from the NER (and LNER) to load the slag for transport to the south for roadmaking.

Torrential rain on 23 July 1930 caused the river Esk to flood and while in spate it demolished a stone bridge in Arncliffe

Woods, just east of Glaisdale. Traffic had to be suspended but after a few days it was resumed from Battersby to Glaisdale in the west, and from Whitby to Egton in the east. Work went on rapidly in designing and erecting a replacement girder bridge and this was opened on 25 May 1931, ready for the summer traffic. Because of the reduction in work at Whitby shed during the winter of 1930-31 three Class F8 2-4-2Ts (490,1577 and 1579) and two J24 0-6-0s (1821 and 1952) were transferred away in October 1930, but when the bridge re-opened Whitby received two J23 0-6-0s (2459 and 2523) and a G5 0-4-4T (1865) all from York.

Only a few months after the new bridge was opened further flooding struck the valley and at the new bridge the river changed its course; after cutting a channel behind one of the abutments the flood-water swept it away completely, leaving the new girder span on the river bed. Once again the line was cut and traffic terminated at Glaisdale on the western side of the break, and at Egton on the eastern side. This time it was decided to re-erect the original span between the bank and a new pier in the centre of the river, and to erect a similar span between the pier and the other bank, over the new course of the river. Work was completed on 27 August 1932, just too late for the summer traffic, and the bridge has given no further trouble.

In 1872 application was made to Parliament for authority to build a line from Brotton to Glaisdale but the Bill was rejected, largely because of opposition from the Whitby, Redcar & Middlesbrough Union Railway, then under construction. However, a similar application in the following year was approved and the Act received the Royal Assent on 7 July 1873, authorising the construction of a line from Brotton to a point on Easington High Moor (5 miles 17 chains) and thence to Glaisdale (5 miles 56 chains). At a point 1 mile 66 chains from the start of the line at Brotton there was to have been a short branch 24 chains long to a pit near Grange Farm on Girrick Moor, some half mile east of the village of Moorsholm. The authorised capital was £170,000 and the line was to have been worked by the North Eastern Railway. Construction of the line was let to the contractor John Waddell of Edinburgh, who also completed the WR&MUR line north of Whitby for the NER, and then went on to build the Scarborough & Whitby Railway. However, shortage of money prevented the line being built from Brotton to Glaisdale, although further Acts were obtained to revive the powers granted under the original Act to the Cleveland Extension Mineral Railway.

Original Act	Revival Act	Period Years	Scheduled Completion Date
7 July 1873	—	5	7 July 1878
—	16 April 1878	3	7 July 1881
—	8 April 1881	3	7 July 1884
—	28 July 1884	3	7 July 1887
—	8 July 1887	3	7 July 1890
—	14 August 1890	3	7 July 1893
—	12 September 1893	3	7 July 1896

Thus the powers extended over twenty three years and still the line was not completed. As the ironworks at Glaisdale closed in 1876 there is no wonder that financial support was not readily forthcoming. In *Bradshaw's Shareholders' Guide* for 1898, in which the Cleveland Extension Mineral Railway is still listed, the chairman is shown as John Preston of 95 Gracechurch Street, London, with W. H. Preston of the same address as one director, and Edward Turner of 4 Harcourt Buildings, Temple, London, as the other. The engineer at that time was J. M. Toler, Saltersford Hall, Holmes Chapel, Cheshire.

The proposed line was to have commenced in the V of the junction between the Lingdale and Kilton branches at Lingdale Junction, some two miles south of Brotton, crossing the moors in a south-easterly direction to Stonegate, some two miles north of Glaisdale. It was then planned to run along the Stonedale Beck valley and to connect with the NER Battersby-Whitby line half a mile on the Battersby side of Glaisdale station. In fact, the ironworks were situated between the proposed junction and the station. Various earthworks are still visible along the course of the line: at Lingdale Junction there is a long shallow cutting and at Liverton Lane end, where the line crossed the Whitby-Guisborough road (now A171), there is a shallow cutting on the north side of the main road and a low embankment on the south. At Stonegate there are signs that a tunnel would have been necessary, and at the southern end of the line a stone overbridge was actually built to carry a minor road over the line near Rake House. This bridge can, in fact, be seen from trains on the Whitby line.

After the closure of the ironworks at Glaisdale, the Extension Railway issued a revised prospectus stressing the

Kildale station, about 1923 (W. Huby).

amount of ironstone available in the area through which the line was planned to pass. It was estimated that there were 20,000 tons of ironstone per acre, and within one mile on each side of the line between Hag Beck and Girrick there were deposits of no less than 80,000,000 tons. The daily traffic was estimated at 3,000 tons per mile but in spite of this glowing report the line still did not attract the necessary capital and it was never built.

The train services on the NY&C when it opened have already been mentioned. By 1900 there were trains from Whitby to Stockton at 6-45 a.m., 8-12 a.m., 10-10 a.m., 1-35 p.m., 3-28 p.m., 5-40 p.m., and 7-55 p.m., and from Stockton to Whitby at 7-42 a.m., 10-49 a.m., 1-50 p.m., 4-13 p.m, 4-45 p.m (starting from Middlesbrough), 5-28 p.m., and 8-5 p.m., all taking about two hours for the 43$\frac{3}{4}$ miles. No trains reversed at Battersby. In the last North Eastern Railway timetable in force from October 1922 the service had been reduced to four trains between Whitby and Stockton (at 10-22 a.m., 1-7 p.m., 3-0 p.m. SO, and 5-32 p.m.) and one between Whitby and Middlesbrough (at 6-55 a.m., via Great Ayton). In the opposite direction trains left Stockton for Whitby at 7-35 a.m., 1-55 p.m., (but this terminated at Battersby Mondays to Fridays), 5-44 p.m., and 8-8 p.m. (Saturdays

Castleton station and its setting (British Railways).

only and only as far as Battersby), together with two from Middlesbrough to Whitby (via Great Ayton) at 10-45 a.m. and 4-40 p.m. At this time the section between Battersby and Picton was also served by the 7-30 a.m. Middlesbrough-Great Ayton-Battersby-Picton-Stockton, and the 10-30 a.m. and 4-15 p.m. in the reverse direction. In the winter of 1934 the departures from Whitby were:-

6-54 a.m.	to Stockton and Ferryhill, via Battersby, Great Ayton and Middlesbrough.
10-22 a.m.	to Stockton via Battersby and Picton.
1-20 p.m.	to Stockton and Ferryhill via Battersby and Picton: steam railcar Mondays to Fridays and steam train Saturdays only.
5-47 p.m.	Whitby-Stockton via Battersby and Picton.
8-00 p.m.	do.

From Stockton trains ran at:-

7-22 a.m.	(actually started from West Hartlepool) via Picton.
10-40 a.m.	via Picton.
1-43 p.m.	steam railcar via Picton: steam train on Saturdays.
4-20 p.m.	via Picton (started from West Hartlepool).
8-15 p.m.	via Picton to Battersby, Saturdays only.

and

6-59 p.m.	Middlesbrough to Whitby via Great Ayton and Battersby.

In addition there were services in both directions between Whitby and Glaisdale.

At the time of closure in June 1954 there were two trains between Whitby and Stockton (via Picton) and two between Whitby and Middlesbrough (via Great Ayton) with the same in the opposite direction, with a Saturdays Excepted Kildale to Whitby train in the morning and a Saturdays only Whitby to Glaisdale in the evening. The line was closed at very short notice and the staff between Battersby and Picton knew nothing of the closure until a day or two before it took place. Thus the service was shown not only in the timetable in force from 14 June 1954 but also in the supplement giving last minute alterations. A Sunday service to and from Whitby was introduced in the 1930s and this was resumed in 1950 but all trains ran via Great Ayton and Battersby.

Pre-1914 some of the services were worked between Stockton

and Whitby by "steam autocars"—namely a Class BTP 0-4-4T and (usually) a couple of coaches with the engine between them. Later the Sentinel steam railcars (of the six cylinder variety) worked the services as part of an intensive roster. For instance in 1937 Stockton No. 430 roster involved:-

	Arrive a.m.	Depart a.m.	
Stockton	—	5-55	Empty
Ferryhill	6-20	6-37	Passenger
Stockton	7-4	7-24	,,
Ferryhill	7-56	8-12	,,
Newcastle	9-30	9-35	Empty
Gateshead shed	9-40	10-24	,,
Newcastle	10-29	10-33	Passenger
Ferryhill	11-46	12-12	,,
Stockton	12-39	1-43	,,
Whitby	3-47	4-25	,,
Goathland	4-55	5-5	,,
Whitby	5-31	5-47	,,
Stockton	7-47	—	

A similar car from the Whitby end worked the 1-20 p.m. from Whitby to Ferryhill and back. Newcastle to Whitby via Leamside, Ferryhill and Stockton in a Sentinel railcar must have been an interesting trip although I doubt if anyone ever performed the through journey!

Closure in 1958 of the coast route between Whitby and Loftus meant that all the Tees-side to Whitby and Scarborough trains had to run via Battersby and reverse there, and in the peak period of the summer of 1958 there were fifteen trains in one direction and fourteen in the other—the largest number of trains the NY&C had seen since it was opened a century earlier. There were even nine trains in each direction on a Sunday. Now (1970-71) there are six trains daily to and from Whitby, with one extra on Saturdays and a further extra daily during the summer. Three trains in each direction also ran on Sundays during the summer months of 1970.

Until December 1925 there was no official published restriction on the engines which could be used on the North Yorkshire & Cleveland between Picton and Grosmont, but on 23 December 1925 severe limitations were imposed between Castleton and Grosmont and only class A6 4-6-2Ts, F8 2-4-2Ts and G5 0-4-4Ts were allowed to work passenger trains. On goods trains only J24 and J25 0-6-0s were permitted. Presumably this was due to the condition of some bridge as the restrictions were lifted from 24 January 1929 and henceforward the largest LNER engines could run as far as Grosmont, beyond which there were restrictions because of the curves and bridges. Thus under the LNER post-war Route Availability scheme the line between Picton and Grosmont became RA 9 (with Groups 8 and 9 restricted to 30 mph) and at the same time Grosmont to Whitby became RA5 but additional classes permitted were D20 and D49 4-4-0; Q6 0-8-0; WD 2-8-0; V1 and V3 2-6-2T; and L1 2-6-4T. Later B1 4-6-0s were allowed and it was 61034 *Chiru* of this class that worked the last passenger train over the Battersby-Picton section on 12 June 1954, on the 6-59 p.m. Battersby to Stockton (5-42 p.m. from Whitby).

5: *Eastwards along the Tees*

THE success of the Stockton & Darlington Railway prompted the company to look round for ways of expanding and it was obvious that the further down river they went the larger the ships that could be handled. Stockton had served its purpose in getting the railway started but the passage up the river Tees was tortuous and slow. Consequently it was decided to extend the line eastwards. An Act for this purpose was obtained on 23 May 1828, with the terminus of the line to be at "Linthorpe otherwise Leventhorpe, or Middlesbrough or Acklam," and although the name Port Darlington was used at first the new terminus became known as Middlesbrough. In 1829 a company was formed to build coal shipping facilities and this concern became known as the Middlesbrough Owners, in which the Pease family played a large part. The company offered a prize of 150 guineas for the best design of a coal shipping staith and this was won by Timothy Hackworth who became better known for his work with Stockton & Darlington locomotives, and his own Soho Works at Shildon. Originally there were drops to load six ships.

The Middlesbrough Owners also planned to develop a new town on the 32 acres of land they had purchased and this was laid out to the south-east of the coal drops. At the time the area chosen for the new town was "little better than a dismal swamp, and the property upon it was little more than a few farm buildings," but from this small start developed the thriving town of Middlesbrough, now included in the Teesside conurbation.

The first train to Middlesbrough on 27 December 1830 was worked by the locomotive *Globe,* newly delivered from Robert Stephenson & Company's works at Newcastle, although designed by Timothy Hackworth. Passengers were conveyed on the inaugural train but the normal service was by a horse-drawn coach: however, in March 1834 instructions were given that six locomotive-worked passenger trains per day were to run between Stockton and Middlesbrough from 7 April 1834, replacing Thomas Harrison's coach, although a horse-drawn coach continued to run on Sundays until the 1850s. The trains terminated at a coach shed just south of the coal drops but in 1837 the shed was moved to a new site on Commercial Street and the service appears to have been worked regularly by the locomotive *Globe,* the boiler of which exploded in the coach station on 18 January 1838. This station was used until 1847 when a new station was opened at Sussex Street on the 1846 extension to Redcar.

The new line from Stockton to Middlesbrough branched off the 1825 line about a mile short of the terminus on Stockton Wharf, at a point now known as Bowesfield Junction, and it immediately crossed the river Tees from County Durham into Yorkshire. This was originally accomplished on a suspension bridge, one of the unwise decisions taken by the Stockton & Darlington Railway, for at that time such bridges were untried for carrying railways. The bridge proved to be unsuitable and in 1841 it was replaced by a bridge of cast-iron girders, strengthened by wrought-iron tension straps, with three river spans of 89 ft. and two shore spans of 31 ft. each. This bridge was replaced in 1907 using the original piers.

When the passenger service was withdrawn from the S&D station at St. John's Crossing, Stockton, in 1848 a station was opened at Thornaby, using the train shed which had just passed out of use at Middlesbrough. This station, known as South Stockton until 1 November 1892, was replaced by the present station from 1 October 1882. The next station was at Newport but the exact date of opening is unknown. In 1875 it had to be demolished to make way for additional tracks. The passenger manager suggested that as the revenue derived from this station was very small it could be closed, but it was decided to keep it open and to provide new station buildings. These remained in use until 8 August 1915, when the station was closed as a wartime measure: after the war it was decided not to reopen it but the platforms remained, straddled by the southern approach spans to the Newport lift bridge for road traffic across the Tees, and occasional excursion traffic was handled until the 1930s.

Between Thornaby and Newport the NER developed extensive sidings and yards, now modernised and known as Tees Yard. These sidings were the eastern terminus of the electrified line from Shildon, which reverted to steam traction in 1935. In the centre of the yards was Newport engine shed, first opened in 1881: being on reclaimed land, extra deep foundations were specified but the building suffered from subsidence and in 1888 it was decided to rebuild the shed on a new site, with increased accommodation. Thus a new building consisting of two roundhouses under one roof was opened in 1890, and this remained in use until 1 June 1958, when it was closed and the stock of engines transferred to the new depot at Thornaby (51L). The sidings which developed on each side of the Stockton to Middlesbrough line eventually led to the diversion of the passenger lines, which were re-routed to pass round the southern extremity of the sidings, and a similar diversion was carried out in 1958 to accommodate the new locomotive shed.

The original industrial development at Middlesbrough took place in the loop of the river immediately to the west of the 1830 coal drops and this area, which at one time was covered with iron and steel works, was served by the Marsh branch, which diverged to the north on the east side of Newport station and connected with the Old Town branch. The latter was originally the route to the coal drops and the coach station. The importance of this area declined when the line was extended to Redcar and greater space became available for developing the ironworks which are still there today.

After a few years operation the Middlesbrough Owners decided to improve their facilities by building a dock to the east of the drops and in November 1838 the S&DR agreed that all coal coming down their line should be shipped from the new dock when it was completed. This occurred in May 1842 and from the twelfth of the month the new dock was open for trade, served by a branch from the line to the station in Commercial Street, diverging at what later became known as Old Town Junction. This branch was built by the Middlesbrough Owners.

The next move was an extension of the railway to Redcar, promoted by a Stockton & Darlington protegee, the Middlesbrough & Redcar Railway. An Act for building the line was obtained on 21 July 1845 and it was opened on 4 June 1846, with the first train hauled by the celebrated *Locomotion No.* 1, followed by the engine A of the Great North of England Railway. The branch actually diverged from the Middlesbrough Dock branch, by this time Stockton & Darlington property, at Dock Hill Junction and adjacent to this point a new Middlesbrough station was built in 1847. This was replaced from 3 December 1877 by the present station, although the magnificent roof had to be demolished in 1942 after being severely damaged by German bombing. In the meantime the

North Eastern Railway had extended the dock and the Middlesbrough Owners had built a connecting line, serving numerous wharfs and sidings, eastwards from the old depots in Commercial Street and along the south bank of the river to join up with the lines on the dock side. A network of lines and sidings to the east of the dock also belonged to the Middlesbrough Owners and their line extended beyond Normanby Ironworks, almost as far as Normanby Jetty. All the Middlesbrough Owners' lines were taken over by the NER in 1884.

The earliest stations between Middlesbrough and Redcar were Cleveland Port and Lazenby, followed by Eston in 1853. However, various renamings and re-sitings have confused the position over the years so each station is dealt with separately:-

Cleveland Port: renamed Cargo Fleet August 1867 and present station opened 8 November 1885.

South Bank: present station opened 1 May 1882.

Eston: at junction of Bolckow Vaughan Eston Mines branch. Opened June 1853: new station approved 10 February 1862 and by September 1874 extensions were necessary. But as the station was incapable of being extended, because it was surrounded by works, a new station at South Bank was proposed. Before this was carried out Eston was renamed South Bank (in January 1878), but when the new South Bank station was opened on 1 May 1882 it reverted to Eston. The station was closed on 22 November 1885 on the opening of Eston Grange (see below).

Eston Grange: opened 22 November 1885. Renamed Grangetown 1 January 1902 and present station dates from 1885.

There was also an Eston station (from 1 January 1902) at the extremity of a short branch off the Cleveland Railway and this will be mentioned later.

Another complication is that on 17 February 1851 the traffic manager of the Stockton & Darlington Railway was authorised to discuss with Messrs. Bolckow Vaughan the possibility of running a train from Middlesbrough to Eston and back over the Bolckow Vaughan line leading to Eston Mines. By 1865 this train was running on Saturday nights only from Eston Mines to Middlesbrough and back, and the NER insisted that while the train was running on Bolckow Vaughan metals it should be run entirely at the iron company's risk, or be discontinued. From 1 May 1873 there were four market trains in each direction between Middlesbrough and Eston Mines on Saturdays, leaving Middlesbrough at 3-0 p.m., 3-40 p.m., 8-0 p.m., and 8-20 p.m., and Eston Mines at 4-10 p.m., 4-35 p.m., 8-25 p.m., amd 8-40 p.m. From notes in the

Middlesbrough station after bombing, August 4th, 1942 (British Railways).

Working Timetable regarding light engine running it would appear that Bolckow Vaughan's locomotives took over between Eston (NER) and Eston Mines, although the NER coaches worked through.

The station at Redcar had a short life because yet again, when it was decided to extend the line to Saltburn, it was found impractical to continue the railway from the original terminus. Thus the 1846 station was left at the end of a spur when the extension to Saltburn was opened. On 16 April 1862 the Stockton & Darlington Railway decided to seek a tenant for the old station buildings, suggesting that they could be used as promenade rooms, and an offer of £40 per annum was received, subject to the railway company carrying out alterations costing approximately £200. Nothing more is known about this project and the next move was on 24 August 1870, when the Darlington Committee of the NER decided that the building should be sold, and posters were issued advertising the sale to be held at the *Swan Hotel,* Redcar, on 15 September 1870. The auctioneer's description read:-

> The Buildings are erected of stone in the most substantial manner, and in the best style. The entrance is screened by an elegant semicircular Portico.
> The site is a most eligible one, being at the intersection of the two principal streets in Redcar; it has two good frontages, one looking direct down the main street of the Town, and the other facing the South. The present Building with but little further outlay could be easily converted into a first-class Hotel. The accommodation consists of a good Entrance Hall, 4 good Rooms, 2 large Halls, each 60 feet by 44 feet, suitable for concert room and sale room, or show room; a Cottage Dwelling behind, containing 4 rooms, and the building formerly used as a Goods Warehouse, which would make an excellent assembly room, or may be converted into stables, with all necessary conveniences, and including about 1,400 square yards of land upon which the building stands.

The property was described as the Central Hall, formerly used as Redcar railway station. It was not sold but was re-offered at another sale, again at the *Swan Hotel,* and again by the auctioneer Mr. Charles Willman, on 20 April 1871. The reserve price of £2,000 was not reached and it was again withdrawn. In June 1873 a Mr. John Cowl offered £2,250 for the property and this was accepted. In May 1864 the extension platform at the old station was removed to the new one on the line to Saltburn. In August 1871 it was ordered that the junction of the old station branch be restored and part of the branch continued to be used as a coal depot into British Railways days. The old station remained standing until the 1960s, part of it in use as a cinema, but it has now been demolished and shops erected on the site.

The extension to Saltburn was authorised by the Stockton & Darlington Act of 23 July 1858 and the new line commenced approximately one mile outside Redcar old station. The new Redcar station was of the single platform type favoured by the S&DR and it was not until 1935 that a separate platform was provided for Saltburn-Darlington trains: from 1 November 1970 it reverted to its original form. There was also an excursion platform on the Middlesbrough side of the station. Originally there was only one intermediate station, at Marske, but Redcar East Halt was opened on 18 May 1929 between Redcar and Marske: the Halt was dropped from the title in 1937. Redcar became Redcar Central in October 1950 but the new title did not appear in the timetable until June 1951. The Redcar-Saltburn line was opened on 17 August 1861, one of its objectives being the ironstone royalties at Skelton, which had just been taken over by Messrs. J. & J. W. Pease, and under the original Act a short branch 47 chains long was authorised to Rushpool Wood. A similar branch was authorised in 1861, to terminate near Marske Mill, but neither line was built.

In the 1850s Saltburn comprised only a few fishermen's cottages, but with the coming of the railway the Stockton & Darlington company decided to develop the area and the Saltburn Improvement Company was formed to build houses and to lay out gardens. In addition the railway company built the *Zetland Hotel* looking out over the sea and the Skelton Beck ravine: the hotel was opened on 27 July 1863 and it is still in use under the control of British Transport Hotels Ltd. An unusual feature was that the hotel was served by an extension of one of the platform lines and this was used for fuel supplies, but this facility was terminated in January 1970.

Now all the stations east of Middlesbrough have become unstaffed halts and they are served by the diesel multiple unit railcars running as pay trains. The service operates approximately every half hour from 05-15 to 22-45, with a journey time of one hour for the 27¾ miles, stopping at all stations. As an economy measure, Marske, Tofts, Saltburn West and Saltburn signalboxes have been closed and Longbeck box, which must remain open to control a level crossing 28 chains west of Marske, has been modernised; it now controls the line to Saltburn and also the junction (formerly controlled by Saltburn West) giving access to the freight only line to Skinningrove.

After a long and bitter struggle with the Stockton & Darlington Railway, the Cleveland Railway managed to reach the Tees at Normanby Jetty on 23 November 1861, crossing the S&DR line from Middlesbrough to Redcar on an overbridge approximately ¾ mile east of Cleveland Port (Cargo Fleet) station. The NER took over the Stockton & Darlington in 1863 and the Cleveland Railway in 1865 and proposals to close the centre section of the Cleveland line followed in 1866. Although powers were obtained in the Cleveland Railway Act of 1861 to connect with the Stockton & Darlington near Cleveland Port station, it was not until the squabbling had died down that this was put in and it was opened in February 1865. Thus when the centre section of the Cleveland Railway was closed it was possible to serve the various mines and sidings from the northern end of the line and, in fact, this continued until October 1966.

Probably because of the difficulty in serving the mining community at Eston over the Bolckow Vaughan Eston Mines branch, the NER decided to build a short $\frac{1}{2}$ mile branch off the former Cleveland Railway at Flatts Lane level crossing, to terminate at a single platform passenger station on the west side of Eston. The necessary powers were incorporated in the NER Act of 6 July 1895 and the line was opened on 1 January 1902. From about 1906 the service was worked by a steam autocar and for the last year or so by a Sentinel steam railcar, until the branch closed to passengers from 11 March 1929: a coal depot remained until the whole of the northern section of the Cleveland line was closed in October 1966.

6: *Some Mines Branches*

A NUMBER of the ironstone mines in the Guisborough area were adjacent to the North Eastern lines and required only short sidings to handle their traffic, but other mines were some considerable distance away from the main lines and needed fully fledged branch lines. Except in a few isolated instances the mines did not own their own locomotives and the traffic was collected by North Eastern locomotives working over the branch, part of which was usually owned by the N.E.R. and part by the mining company. These branches, some of which were as much as two miles long, were operated under the "staff" method of working, whereby the driver carried a metal (usually brass) token. Possession of the "staff" allowed his train, and no other, to work on the branch.

The longest branch worked in this way was that to Chaloner Mines, 2 miles 23 chains in length, of which 58 chains, from the junction with the Middlesbrough & Guisborough Railway just west of Pinchinthorpe station, were North Eastern property and the remaining 1 mile 45 chains the property of Bolckow, Vaughan & Co. (later Dorman, Long & Co. Ltd.). The branch was originally connected with the Cleveland Railway but when the centre section of the Cleveland was closed it could be reached only from the Guisborough end. In 1873 this eastern section of the Cleveland Railway was abandoned and the Chaloner branch extended about ½ mile southwards to connect with the former Middlesbrough & Guisborough Railway line. The branch crossed a minor road north of Pinchinthorpe and, running in a north-easterly direction, then crossed the main road from Guisborough to Middlesbrough (now A171). Until a few years ago a small crossing-keeper's hut stood at this point but after slowly deteriorating for many years it was finally demolished, although there are still traces of it on the roadside. Chaloner Mines were situated on the west side of a minor road running north-westwards from Guisborough to Wilton, and although the mines worked until 1939 the outlet via the North Eastern had been out of use for many years. This was because in 1879 the mine workings were linked with those at Upsall, further to the west, and the ironstone could then reach the furnaces via the owner's Eston inclines. In 1916 a surface line connected Chaloner with the Eston system: this ran the opposite way, round the eastern fold of the hills, and the branch to the N.E.R. was removed not long afterwards.

Next in length was the branch from Slapewath to Skelton Park Pit, 1 mile 73 chains long, of which 36 chains were owned by the North Eastern and the remaining 1 mile 37 chains by the mining company. This shaft was opened in 1872 by Bell Bros., but passed into the hands of Dorman, Long in 1923. The line closed in 1938 and it was dismantled in the following year. This branch was actually an extension of the line from Slapewath to Skelton Pit, the first shaft mine in Cleveland, opened in 1861 when the Cleveland Railway first provided easy transport to the Tees. Soon after leaving the N.E.R., the branch crossed the Guisborough-Whitby road (A171) on an overbridge (of which the foundations can still be located on the south side of the road) and then ran northwards to Skelton Park mine situated ¼ mile south of the Guisborough-Skelton road (A173): the mine buildings can still be seen from the latter road. About 500 yards from the junction with the N.E.R. there was a tipping point serving a line which ran from Waterfall Mine, about ½ mile away to the north-west, but this mine had a life of only twenty years or so and ceased operations in 1901.

On the opposite side of the Guisborough-Brotton line, to the east of the A171 overbridge, two branches went off to the south, both just short of a mile in length. First came the line to Slapewath Mines, which passed under the old course of the main road at Charltons village: the present course of the road runs to the east of the village and it is possible to see the bridge from the new road. This branch, 71 chains long, was owned by Sir B. Samuelson & Co. and ceased operations in 1906, although ironstone continued to be taken out through Spawood Mines which were nearer the N.E.R.

A short distance further to the east the Aysdalegate branch diverged from the North Eastern, running southwards but keeping on the east side of the main road, to terminate in the bend at the foot of the hill, Birk Brow, where a row of miners' cottages still stands. The first record of this line is dated 15 November 1875, when the N.E.R. were requested to provide a junction for the branch: this was authorised on 31 August 1876 but on 3 September 1879 instructions were given that the junction should be removed, together with the nearby junction

Cleveland byways. Top: Train crossing Flatts Lane, Ormesby, on remains of old Cleveland Railway, September 13th, 1960. Bottom: Lingdale Junction, May 21st, 1959, with lines to Kilton Mine on left and Lingdale Mine on right. Kilton shaft and pit-heap is on the far left.

to Slapewath Mines. It appears that both junctions were reinstated at some later date, as Aysdalegate is known to have worked until at least 1903. It also seems probable that both Aysdalegate and Slapewath branches were worked by horses as neither line appears in North Eastern records as one over which N.E.R. engines were allowed to work.

A mile south of Brotton the Kiltonthorpe Railway diverged from the N.E.R. line to Guisborough, running 1 mile 21 chains south-eastwards to mines opened at Kilton in 1870. This branch was privately built by Mr. J. T. Wharton, the owner of the land, and Messrs. Robson, Cochrane & Co., the lessee of the mining rights. As early as September 1872 Mr. Wharton advised the North Eastern that he was willing to sell the line for £10,000 and Mr. Harrison, the North Eastern's engineer, was instructed to investigate and report back. This he did on 27 September 1872, stating that the line occupied a portion of the route which would be required for any extension of the N.E.R. towards the Liverton district and he recommended its purchase. The directors accepted his report and instructed Mr. Bell, to commence negotiations with Mr. Wharton. The branch opened on 11 June 1873. In the same year the N.E.R. applied for powers to take over the Kiltonthorpe Railway and these were granted in the Act of 16 July 1874, although the North Eastern had worked the branch from the outset. Coal cells were built at Kiltonthorpe where the Loftus-Lingdale road passed under the line: the bridge at this point has now been demolished.

At this same location Lingdale Junction was established for the 1 mile 32 chains branch to Lingdale Mines opened in 1878 by Pease & Partners. The line was the property of the mine owners, running on land again owned by Mr. J. T. Wharton, who received a wayleave on the ironstone passing over the branch. The amount of the wayleave varied between ½d. and 1½d. per ton, dependent on the current price of pig iron. The branch was leased by the North Eastern under an agreement of 4 July 1896, but only under a sub-letting arrangement with Pease & Partners. Ironstone traffic ceased in 1931 but the L.N.E.R. worked an occasional wagon of stores up to Lingdale, until in July 1940 it was decided to re-habilitate and reopen the line. The 1896 lease continued in force but new wayleave rates were negotiated and the line operated in this way until the lease was terminated in November 1963. Thus the Lingdale branch was never the property of the N.E.R., L.N.E R., or B.R. although worked by their locomotives and men. Lingdale Mines closed on 23 February 1962 and Kilton Mines on 2 February 1963, and both the Kiltonthorpe and Lingdale

Bridge near Skelton showing effects of mining subsidence. The bridge had to have a lower arch added for strengthening purposes.

branches have been removed.

At one time a small wooden signal box was provided at the junction of the Lingdale branch with the Kiltonthorpe line and it was here that a mineral train was derailed on 5 November 1900. The engine, No. 1245 of Class 1001, finished up almost completely upside down on the bank side on the west side of the line, surrounded by wrecked wagons. Two steam cranes were required to get the engine and tender back on the lines. Dorman, Long & Co. Ltd. took over Kilton Mines (from Bell Bros.) in 1923, and Lingdale Mines (from Pease & Partners) in 1952. Small diesel locomotives were introduced in 1951 for underground haulage at Kilton and at closure there were more than thirty such locomotives at work at Kilton and Lingdale, with a further ten at North Skelton, also a Dorman, Long mine latterly. North Skelton was actually the last ironstone mine to work in Cleveland and closed on 17 January 1964.

Another long branch was that to Upleatham Mines, 1 mile 62 chains, of which 39 chains were owned by the North Eastern and 1 mile 23 chains by Pease & Partners. The branch ran almost due south from the N.E.R. at Blacks Bridge, which carries the Eston-Marske road (A171) over the Middlesbrough-Saltburn line. It passed close to the village of New

Marske, which was built to house the mineworkers and their families, and terminated at the mines on the hillside south of the village. The mines, in three parts, were closed from 1912, until the last section closed in 1923: the branch was removed soon afterwards.

A short branch, but one which lasted until British Railways' days, was the Normanby branch, which left the northern section of the truncated Cleveland Railway at Deans Siding. This siding was on the east side of the Normanby -Guisborough road (Flatts Lane) which was crossed on the level by two tracks unprotected by gates. The only warning given of approaching trains was by the guard holding a red flag to stop road traffic. The southern track across the road was originally the main line of the Cleveland Railway, latterly serving the Normanby brick and tile works, and the northern track was the Normanby branch. The latter served Normanby Mines, and terminated at Ormesby Mines, almost $\frac{3}{4}$ mile along the foot of the hills. The system closed down on 3 October 1966, although latterly the only traffic was bricks as both mines had closed many years earlier.

7: *Engines*

BECAUSE of the intensity of the rail traffic on Teesside it required five locomotive depots to supply the engines! in addition, engines worked into the area from York, Leeds, Darlington, West Hartlepool, Scarborough, Shildon, Gateshead and Whitby. In 1914 the sheds, with the number of engines stationed there, and the number of men employed, were:—

SHED	ENGINES	MEN
Middlesbrough	85	369
Newport	100	403
Stockton	52	217
Haverton Hill	12	66
Saltburn	15	37

Three circular sheds—roundhouses—were built at Middlesbrough between 1866 and 1872 and housed engines for working both passenger and freight trains, as well as supplying engines for shunting on the docks. The passenger engines were mainly small tank engines for working local passenger services, and the goods and mineral engines were of North Eastern classes C,P, and P1 of the 0–6–0 wheel arrangement.

Later T and T1 0–8–0 engines proved extremely useful in the area, and as they were scrapped in the 1940s they were replaced by the larger T2 class (LNER Q6). By the 1930s the shed buildings were in a bad state of repair and those that had not fallen down were demolished in 1959 and 1960. The engines had by then been transferred to the new shed at Thornaby.

Newport shed housed only freight and mineral engines and in 1939, out of an allocation of 112 engines, 101 were 0–6–0s and 0–8–0s: the remaining 11 were shunting tank engines. The shed consisted of two roundhouses under one roof and it was closed in 1958 when the engines were transferred to Thornaby. It was demolished soon afterwards to make room for extensions to the marshalling yard.

Stockton was an eight-road straight shed opened in 1891,

replacing a smaller shed alongside the old station: this shed had to be demolished to make way for the extensions to the station, completed in 1893. The new shed housed mainly freight engines, with a smattering of 2–4–2T and 0–4–4T for local passenger workings. In British Railways days the shed received a stud of B1 4–6–0s for working braked goods trains, chiefly to York, but these engines were also used during the summer months to work over the difficult and hilly road to Scarborough.

About 1905 seven P1 0–6–0 engines (Nos. 459, 463, 1714, 1986, 2034, 2041, and 2133) were fitted with vacuum brake apparatus and stationed at Stockton shed to work trains made up of 30 ton ironstone wagons also fitted with the vacuum brake. Altogether 260 four-wheel hopper wagons were built for the Cleveland ironstone traffic but it was found that the time gained on the banks, by having control of the whole train, was lost in coupling and uncoupling and the vacuum brake equipment was removed from the wagons between 1916 and 1919. In the meantime, in 1912, trials had been carried out on ironstone trains from Upleatham and Spawood using engine 2041 and the N.E.R. dynamometer car.

Thirty ton, forty ton, and even fifty ton bogie ironstone wagons were considered in 1904 but the 50 ton wagon was rejected as not feasible. Consideration was given to the bogie 30 ton (costing £160) and the bogie 40 ton (costing £240) but it was decided that a 30 ton wagon on four wheels would be more suitable and the bogie wagon ideas were shelved. These all metal hopper wagons were designed to carry thirty tons of hot calcined ironstone from Liverton Mines but they were also used for unburnt stone from the other mines. The dimensions were similar to the more familiar 23 ton wooden bodied hopper wagons used for coal traffic, with a length over headstocks of 20′ 0″, height above rail level 9′ 10″, and extreme width 8′ 0″. The tare weight was 12 tons 12 cwt.

Saltburn shed was primarily a passenger engine shed, providing locomotives for trains to Darlington and along the coast to Scarborough. For many years the engines used were the useful Class O 0–4–4T, but the Class D (LNER H1) 4–4–4T started to appear in 1913. In the fifteen years they spent at Saltburn the Class D engines were not satisfactory and in 1928–30 they were replaced by eight of the Hawthorn, Leslie & Co. built A5 4–6–2Ts, based on a Great Central Railway design. By 1939 all the H1 4–4–4Ts had been rebuilt as 4–6–2Ts and reclassified A8: in their new form Saltburn received seven of these engines in exchange for the A5 locomotives and they put in a lot of hard work in the area, particularly on the half-hourly service between Saltburn, Middlesbrough and Darlington. Smaller sheds (mentioned in the text) existed at various times at Guisborough, Carlin How, Battersby and Rosedale.

For many years one class of engine which could be found on Cleveland traffic was the famous Stockton & Darlington long-boilered 0–6–0 of Class 1001, although the classification was nominal and covered a variety of generally similar engines. These were built by various locomotive building firms, as well as at Darlington Works, and the last appeared in 1875: No. 1275 of the class, one of the 1874 built engines, ran until 1923 and it was the only one which lasted long enough to pass into the hands of the L.N.E.R. It took part in the Railway Centenary Procession from Stockton to Darlington in July 1925 and since then it has been preserved in the Railway Museum at York. These were followed by the Class C (LNER J21) 0–6–0s designed by T. W. Worsdell, the first of which appeared in 1886, but the most successful engines in Cleveland were undoubtedly the Wilson Worsdell P and P1 classes (LNER J24 and J25) which first appeared in 1894 and 1898 respectively. Altogether 190 of these P and P1 engines were built and in 1923 there were 35 at work in the Cleveland area.

It is surprising how few privately owned locomotives worked in the district. In fact the only mine to possess a standard gauge shunter appears to have been Liverton, where a 0–4–0ST was used. One or two companies used narrow gauge systems and engines to haul the ore from the mines to the tipping point and two companies near Great Ayton each used a narrow gauge Lewin locomotive on their whinstone quarrying operations. Glaisdale, Grosmont and Skinningrove ironworks each maintained a fleet of standard gauge locomotives for shunting operations within their works, and Bolckow, Vaughan (later Dorman, Long) engines were used to haul ironstone from the foot of the inclines at Eston to the ironworks two miles to the north. At Grinkle Park the 3′ 0″ gauge system started life with three Black, Hawthorn 0–4–0Ts built in 1872 and a few years later two engines were obtained from John Fowler & Co. of Leeds. Finally, prior to World War I, two 0–4–0STs were bought from Hudswell,Clark & Co., also of Leeds. The Fowler and Hudswell, Clark engines lasted until the equipment was disposed of about 1934.

8: *Stations*

THE most attractive station in Cleveland, to my mind, was that at Guisborough, with its overall roof and unusual glass end screens. Adjoining was the solid stone built house for the stationmaster, with its Stockton & Darlington Railway house plaque lettered B12 just under the eaves on the eastern wall. The passenger services ceased in March 1964, followed by the freight services in August of the same year and now the station and house have both gone and in their place has appeared a brick box labelled Health Centre. This looks out of place as, although there has been extensive housing development on the outskirts of the town, the centre has changed little except for a so called modern post office, and a few new shop fronts.

The battered remnants of Middlesbrough are still there in all their grimy magnificence. Destruction of the roof in the 1942 air-raid has necessitated undistinguished platform awnings—and I wonder if the subway is any cleaner than when I last used it? The station was opened in December 1877 and the tenders for its construction amounted to £69,382 1s 2d. Perhaps N.E.R. station buildings were made to last too long? Middlesbrough is nearly a century old and should have been replaced years ago.

To go to the other end of the scale: what better site could there be for a station than Sandsend? Because of the hills and the streams it had to be built on the cliff side at the northern end of the village. To think that the stationmaster had to be paid to live there, with an unobstructed view across the North Sea from his front window, the sea shore only a few feet below him, and trains at his door! The station, the sea, and the shore are still there but the trains deserted the station in 1958, when the 4–20 pm from Middlesbrough called at 5–59 pm (five minutes late) on 3 May carrying the last passengers to and from Sandsend.

Skinningrove, Grinkle and North Skelton stations have all but disappeared and can now only be located by a few grassy mounds, while other stations have survived but have been

Exterior of the now demolished Guisborough station, August 26th, 1966. Note the Stockton & Darlington house number plaque under the eaves on the top left-hand corner of the end wall.

reduced in size. Kildale, for instance, now has only one platform and that has been considerably reduced in length. Potto is still a residence but little altered from its N.E.R. days, whereas Hutton Gate, as mentioned previously, is now a very attractive house standing in its own grounds (formerly the station yard and the site of the platforms). Brotton, Stokesley, and the major part of Loftus stations still exist, and the latter is to see trains once again when the potash traffic from the new mine at Boulby starts up. Many people must have gone to live near the line between Carlin How and Boulby, little thinking that one day their solitude would be broken by snarling diesel locomotives hauling wagons loaded with potash!

Quite the most disappointing station in the area is Battersby. It has a poor range of buildings and bare platforms for what was once a busy station, especially with interchange traffic between Whitby-Stockton and Battersby-Middlesbrough trains. Of course it was really an afterthought, built only $\frac{3}{4}$ mile east of Ingleby, its position decided by the Rosedale branch junction, which was not included in the early plans of the North Yorkshire & Cleveland Railway. Not far away is Ingleby Incline, but unfortunately it cannot be seen from Battersby.

However, it is still worth a visit, if only to see to what lengths the North Eastern Railway was prepared to go to get the ironstone traffic, especially when one of the mine owners was the deputy chairman of the railway company, and another the traffic manager. Now all ore has to be imported and perhaps it is appropriate that the Tees is to accommodate a large new ore terminal to handle the ore for all the steelworks in the north east.

Sandsend station, viewed from footplate of engine working Scarborough-Middlesbrough train on the last day the line was open, May 3rd, 1958.